Contents

Abbreviations   vii

1. Faith   1

2. Intolerance   15

3. Charity   43

4. Hope   73

5. Disappointment   103

6. Desperation   124

Suggested Further Reading   147

Notes   148

Index   150

The men and women of your class — tell them their
      wrongs and yours —
Plant in their hearts that hatred deep that suffers and
      endures,
And treasuring up each deed of wrong, each scornful
      word and look,
Inscribe it in the memory, as others in a book
And wait and watch through toiling years the ripening
      of time,
Yet deem to strike before that hour were worse than
      folly — crime!

             from JAMES CONNOLLY, 'The Legacy'[1]

To Michael Kersse

Abbreviations

AFL	American Federation of Labor
BSP	British Socialist Party
BTUC	British Trades Union Congress
DORA	Defence of the Realm Act
GEB	General Executive Board (of IWW)
ICA	Irish Citizen Army
ILP	Independent Labour Party
ILP(I)	Independent Labour Party of Ireland
INL	Irish National League
IRB	Irish Republican Brotherhood
ISF	Irish Socialist Federation
ISRP	Irish Socialist Republican Party
ITGWU	Irish Transport and General Workers' Union
ITUC	Irish Trades Union Congress
IWW	Industrial Workers of the World
NEC	National Executive Committee (of SLP)
SDF	Social Democratic Federation
SLP	Socialist Labour Party
SPA	Socialist Party of America
SPI	Socialist Party of Ireland
SSF	Scottish Socialist Federation
ST&LA	Socialist Trade & Labor Alliance
TUC	Trades Union Congress

Acknowledgments

I should like to acknowledge with gratitude the help I have received in writing this book. Members of the staff of the National Library of Ireland (particularly Dónall Ó Luanaigh) showed me great kindness. Oliver Snoddy pointed out a neglected source. My parents gave me advice on sources and encouragement throughout and made helpful comments on the typescript. My husband, John Mattock, improved my prose considerably and with Michael Kersse provided practical help and cheered me on at all stages. My brother Owen gave me the benefit of his many years of research and thought on Connolly, made some very useful suggestions on sources, lent me books and spent much time and effort on my typescript, offering numerous invaluable and constructive criticisms. My publishers were efficient and helpful, and my editor, Colm Croker, did a superb job in picking up errors and obscurities.

1
Faith

1

The material circumstances into which James Connolly was born were appalling — enough to implant resentment in the sturdiest child, to yield bitter fruit in the most phlegmatic adult years later; his parents, John and Mary (*née* McGinn), were among many Catholic emigrants living the slum life in the Cowgate, one of the Irish Catholic ghettoes of Edinburgh, when Mary bore him, her third son, on 5 June 1868. The Cowgate had the distinction among the city's slums of having the worst living conditions and the highest unemployment. John was then at work carting human and household waste for the Corporation, a job he held, except for a brief period as a lamplighter, until 1889, when, after an accident at the age of fifty-six, he was made caretaker at a public convenience. His wage of 19s 6d per week was reduced to 7s 6d. Long before that the three boys were out at work as a matter of necessity.

By the time James left St Patrick's School in the Cowgate at the age of ten or eleven his eldest brother, John, had already joined the British army and been sent to India, and Thomas, the next, of whom little is known, had apparently been in printing work prior to permanent emigration. Young James was faced with a series of exhausting and dispiriting dead-end jobs of the sort that had driven his brother and so many of his peers and contemporaries through desperation into the British army. He was first a printer's devil (fired when an inspector discovered his age), then a bakery hand, where the length of the hours and the physical demands of the job proved too much for a twelve-year-old boy. His intense hatred of the place led him from it to a mosaic tiling factory, whose policy of employing cheap juvenile labour had him dismissed, it would seem, as too old at the age of fourteen. In 1882, for want of better alternatives, he falsified his age and name and followed his brother into the British army, possibly joining the Royal Scots Regiment.

Even at this age the new recruit had unusual qualities. Many of his fellows, of course, were of equally impoverished origin and carried the social burden of first- and second-generation immigrants, harried by the prejudice of the natives into a heightened sense of their Irish Catholic origins. There was no lack of Irish nationalists from British slums in the ranks of the Empire's army; the land agitation was at its height, Parnell had been jailed under the coercion laws, and the murder of two government officials in Phoenix Park had intensified anti-Irish xenophobia among the mainland British. No product of an Irish community could be unaware of the political tensions of the period. Yet James Connolly's awareness was of a different order from the mass of his fellows. His father, though not a politically inclined man, was intelligent and — unusually for his time and background — literate and tolerant. He would have been likely to encourage rather than oppose the obsessive desire for self-education which was emerging in his youngest son. As a child, James had read by the light of embers and used charred sticks as pencils, and this infant precocity and single-mindedness led him to an avid reading, even before he joined the army, of the publications of the Irish Land League.

He used his free time as a soldier to learn about history, politics, economics and socialism. If he was already sympathetic to nationalism in the early 1880s, he emerged at the end of the decade a believer in [3] radical socialism, his original political nationalism having been reinforced by the experiences he had undergone in the service of the Queen. (We know little about those seven years, for the petty prejudices he encountered later in his life as a political agitator in Ireland and Irish communities in America discouraged him from reminiscing about his birthplace and his army service — to the extent that for decades after his death he was believed to have been born in Ulster and to have been in various manual jobs throughout the 1880s. We know, though, that he served in Ireland, and possibly in Scotland and India,[2] and some of his later writings suggest that he almost certainly saw action, possibly participating in a bayonet charge. He later told an intimate how his festering hatred of the British army was exacerbated by being forced to spend a night in Ireland guarding a man about to be executed, on dubious evidence, for his part in an agrarian massacre.)

There were compensations. Connolly developed during this period what was to prove a fateful affection for Dublin, and there fell in love with a gentle Protestant girl, Lillie Reynolds, a domestic servant in a Unionist family. By the spring of 1889 they were engaged and it appears that on hearing the news of his father's accident (with its implications for his chronically sick mother) he went AWOL from his unit.

It was not until April 1890 that James and Lillie were in a position to marry, for he had first to find a job, and at a period of high unemployment. Without educational qualifications, intelligence and wide general reading were irrelevant, and radical political opinions were, if voiced, a deterrent to employers. James could compete only for manual work, where his reliability and longstanding teetotalism at least would count in his favour. After a year in Dundee he settled in Edinburgh, following his father's old occupation of night-soil man. (His brother John, also back from soldiering, did the same. If anything, he was more fortunate: he had steady Corporation employment, while James was with a private firm and subject to periodical lay-offs. Either way, the social necessity of the work did nothing to alleviate its revolting nature or the social stigma attached to it.) James and Lillie were able to set up a modest home, free for a while, at least from the crippling financial burdens that were to be a feature of their married life.

[4]

2

James Connolly was now almost twenty-two and ready, ideologically and temperamentally, to begin his involvement with active socialism. Up to now he had acquired his knowledge and developed his political ideas almost in isolation, but his new life was to give him the opportunity to learn in a more disciplined way — through directed reading and private and public discussion with companions who could assist his intellectual development. In the year he spent in Dundee before his marriage he had attended some socialist meetings and had met John Leslie, a gifted speaker and writer, a man of wide reading and sympathetic personality and a friend of James's socialist brother John. He was the first secretary of the Scottish Socialist Federation (SSF), founded in 1888 and based mainly in Edinburgh. Connolly joined in 1890.

British socialists were deeply divided at the time. The British Social Democratic Federation (SDF), a Marxist organisation, had split in 1884 because a number of its leaders, including the poet and artist William Morris, and Edward Aveling, Karl Marx's son-in-law, had come to believe that the movement should confine itself to pure propaganda and eschew any involvement with the parliamentary system. These dissenters set up the breakaway Socialist League, which denounced as 'opportunist' the policy of the SDF and its founder and leader, Henry Hyndman, of making alliances and compromises with political parties to secure reforms. Many rank and file of both bodies regretted the split and indeed held dual membership. The SSF was founded to accommodate Scottish socialists who sought unity.

The people he met through the SSF — and Leslie in particular — were to give Connolly the opportunity to apply his logical, quick and powerful mind to the disciplined study of Marxist theory and its application to his twin preoccupations — Irish nationalism and social inequality. Through its study groups he acquired a thorough grounding in, and understanding of, the sparse and often difficult socialist literature that existed at the time. He took every possible advantage of the help it offered. While many members of the SSF study groups were content with popular socialist writing, Connolly applied himself steadily to reading more difficult Marxist classics, even, apparently, picking up some French and German to widen the field of his studies.

In spite of his job, then, his first five years back in Edinburgh were intellectually stimulating. He could afford a tenement large enough for small socialist discussion meetings as well as his growing family, three of whom, Mona, Nora and Aideen, were born before the Connollys left the city. He normally attended at least three weekly SSF meetings: the Sunday public meeting, the midweek lecture and the Friday informal discussion. From an early stage he was additionally drawn into the activities of the Independent Labour Party (ILP), of which John Leslie became Edinburgh secretary. The ILP was founded in 1893 (although the

Edinburgh branch of its predecessor, the Scottish
[6] Labour Party, had been known as the ILP for several
years previously) by Keir Hardie, the man who more
than anyone else shaped the political history of the
labour movement. Its primary aim was simply to represent the voice of the working classes in politics;
unlike the SSF, it had little interest in scientific socialism. The two organisations worked well and flourished
together during the early 1890s, the SSF's propaganda
work bringing recruits both to it and the ILP, while
the ILP's steady organisational work and increasing
popular support brought it more closely in touch with
the trade union movement.

Connolly was not content simply to learn and
think. He was already a respected organiser and
administrator and was beginning to make a name as a
speaker. Not overnight, however. He had first to over-
come his handicaps — his youth, the demands of his
job, the long absence from Edinburgh which had cut
him off from people and developments there, his lack
of formal education, and his physical appearance. With
confidence and age he became a commanding figure,
but in his first years in socialist circles he had much
to compensate for. Though sturdily built, he was only
five and a half feet tall, rather bow-legged (possibly
the result of malnutrition as a child), and he suffered
from short sight, a squint and, until determination
quelled it, a stammer. His Edinburgh working-class
accent was to cause him problems in Ireland and
America. While still in his early twenties, though,
he had the tenacity and conviction to surmount personal obstacles by sheer will-power and application,
and taught himself, by laborious trial and painful
error, to reach through the written and spoken word
the minds and hearts of many people. It was not an
easy mission for Connolly or his associates. The
general public was ignorant about socialism, while the

churches, the politicians and most of the press were actively hostile. The task of winning recruits was arduous and often cheerless, and there were few radicals of the commitment or intellectual calibre to absorb socialist teaching and relate it pragmatically to the concerns of the disaffected mass, who must ultimately provide the base for political success. Connolly soon proved himself an invaluable propagandist.

His first published writing appeared in the Social Democratic journal, *Justice,* in 1892, when he became secretary of the SSF and furnished regular branch reports. His trenchant style was a direct reflection of his aggressive and plain-speaking personality; there are those who learn from experience that ornate prose is often less effective than blunt assertion and adjust accordingly, but Connolly, a talented primitive, never went though that stage. To readers who had much to endure from writers who addressed them in lofty or difficult words, the natural power, translucence and humour of his writing was attractive.

An early contribution to *Justice* triumphantly announced that the SSF had had conspicuous success in gaining public support in Edinburgh — a city

> largely composed of snobs, flunkeys, mashers, lawyers, students, middle-class pensioners and dividend-hunters. Even the working-class portion of the population seemed to have imbibed the snobbish would-be respectable spirit of their 'betters'. But it [socialism] has won, hands down, and is now becoming respectable.

This emboldened him to try to set up an SSF branch in Leith, which as an industrial centre

> having its due proportion of sweaters, slave-drivers, rack-renting slum landlords, shipping-federation agents, and parasites of every description

might be expected to respond well to the socialist
[8] message. He was almost ready to spread his wings
beyond the confines of his native city.

3

Although Connolly's progress was fast, he was yet to
develop originality as a thinker. He was concentrating on understanding Marxist dogma and applying it
practically and along orthodox lines to the Scotland
of his day. His nationalism was undefined and secon-
dary to his socialist activities; it was to be some time
before he hibernicised the ideology of class struggle.
The process began during 1894.

When Connolly joined the army in 1882 Parnell
had been a unifying force in Irish politics. Under his
banner marched not only the largely middle-class supporters of Home Rule but also the great bulk of the
impoverished tenant farmers of Ireland pressing for
land reforms. With Parnell as its president, the Irish
National Land League had forced many concessions
from both the Liberal government and individual landlords themselves. Parnell's success during the 1880s,
through an alliance with Gladstone's Liberals, in gaining government support for a measure of Home Rule
for Ireland, coupled with further land reforms, took
the heat out of Irish politics. Mounting Irish confidence in Parnell verged on the idolatrous, and so
there was little opportunity for the left to get any
agitation going on the land question. The landless
peasantry, who at the height of the Land League's
power had been actively involved in politics, lost
interest, and Parnellite supporters came to be more
and more representative of the *petite bourgeoisie.*

Unity gave way to internecine disputes when Parnell's party split in 1890 after his citation in a divorce
case. He died in the following year, and the debate on

the future of Ireland was thrown open again. The Edinburgh socialists, with their large Irish member- ship, began to focus their attention on the activities of the Edinburgh branch of the Irish National League (INL), the successor to the Land League. The INL was a powerful electoral organisation dedicated to constitutional reform, with land reform second (unlike the Land League, which had reverse priorities), and was largely under the domination of the Irish Parliamentary Party. Its fortunes took a downward turn after Parnell's fall. Although the Liberals, with Irish support, managed to scrape back to power in 1892, the bitter divisions within the Irish Party were reflected in the INL. The alliance with the Liberals had always made radical supporters uneasy, as had the concomitant 'bourgeoisification' of the party and the INL. Connolly, like many socialists, had continued to hope that Ireland would benefit from the activities of the parliamentary nationalists (though he was later to see its successes in achieving land reforms chiefly as a necessary and inevitable step in the historical process — making Ireland capitalist). By 1893, however, the INL became a target for socialist opposition. Without unity in its leadership it could no longer expect to avoid outright challenge from its left.

Connolly was still too immature politically to take a lead in a major reassessment of the 'Irish question'; that job fell to John Leslie, himself half Irish. The experience of seeing the INL supporting the Liberal against the ILP candidate in the Edinburgh municipal elections of 1893 led Leslie to undertake that reassessment in a series of articles published in *Justice* during 1894. It appeared later the same year as a pamphlet entitled *The Present Position of the Irish Question*. Leslie, like Michael Davitt (creator of the Land League), saw the Parnellite—Liberal alliance in retrospect as a sell-out of the mass of the Irish people, sub-

ordinating their needs to the Home Rule movement,
[10] but he retained enough respect for Parnell, 'a Titan strangled by pygmies', to mourn his downfall. Without him there was no reason for the Irish masses to continue to support the party, all of whose factions were led by 'gintlemen'. The only hope for the common people was to put their faith in the achievement through socialism of an Ireland industrialised but fair. This was the moment to establish there an independent party of the peasantry and, more particularly, the growing urban proletariat.

Leslie's ideas, which he had propounded in lectures to SSF members during 1893, had an immediate and profound effect on Connolly. In 1894, in his capacity as secretary of the Central Edinburgh branch of the ILP, Connolly wrote to Keir Hardie urging him to make a strong anti-monarchical, anti-capitalist speech at a Dublin meeting, with the object of encouraging growth in the Irish labour movement. The opposing factions of the Irish Parliamentary Party, he said, were essentially middle-class:

> Their advanced attitude upon the land question is simply an accident arising out of the exigencies of the political situation, and would be dropped to-morrow if they did not realise the necessity of linking the Home Rule agitation to some cause more clearly allied to their daily wants than a mere embodiment of national sentiment of the people.[3]

It was an assured and well-written letter and shows how far Connolly had developed in only four years as an active socialist. Only twenty-six years old, he had achieved so much respect as a speaker and organiser that the SSF preferred him to John Leslie as their candidate in the St Giles ward in the city council elections of November 1894. His background gave him a

good chance of wresting Irish support from Liberal
to socialist.

Connolly fought the election mainly on local hous-
ing conditions. He appealed to the Irish voters to see

> that the landlord who grinds his peasants on a Con-
> nemara estate, and the landlord who rack-rents
> them in a Cowgate slum, are brethren in fact and
> deed.

They must realise, he declared, that Liberals and Conservatives were members of the same party of property.
One opponent, Gardiner, attacked him as a 'young
man of no business ability advocating ideas repugnant
to all right-thinking men', and the INL, of course,
urged the Irish to vote for the official Liberal. Another
major disadvantage was that the most fertile ground
for canvassing was among the very poor, many of
whom were voteless 'lodgers'.

Despite his handicaps, the sheer energy and vitality
of Connolly's campaign won him a great deal of attention and support. His open-air meetings gained large
audiences, and he won just over 14 per cent of the
total poll, a creditable achievement about which he
waxed optimistic in the regular column (appropriately
called 'Plain Talk') he was by now writing for a local
left-wing paper under the pseudonym 'R. Ascal'. The
omens for the future were good, he believed. The
official Liberal, for all his party machine, managed to
obtain a majority of only four to one

> over a party the most revolutionary and the most
> recent in public life, with no electioneering organi-
> sation, and with a candidate known to earn his
> bread by following an occupation most necessary
> in our city life, but nevertheless universally despised
> by the public opinion of aristocratic Edinburgh.

Ultimate victory was assured, he maintained. Until
[12] then

> Every fresh seat captured must simply be regarded
> as a fresh means of spoiling the little games of the
> Jabezian philanthropists, financial jobbers, and poli-
> tical thimbleriggers, who thrive on their reputations
> as Liberal and Tory politicians.

4

For all his growing success in public life, Connolly
was as vulnerable to fluctuations in the labour market
as those whose lives he was seeking to transform. During the severe winter of 1894 the city council dis-
pensed with the use of private contractors for refuse
collection and he was out of work. Edinburgh politics
was one thing, but he had to provide for his family.
He opened a cobbler's shop and quickly proved the
truth of Gardiner's jibe about his lack of commercial
acumen. He had no talent for cobbling either, and he
quit the business in May 1895. Walking out, he said,
to buy a looking-glass to watch himself starve to death,
he began to look around, from his position as secretary
of the SSF, for paid work as an organiser or propagandist.

There were also disappointments in his political
activities. Standing again for St Giles's ward in the
April Poor Law elections, he was handsomely defeated
by a local priest, and he was bitterly upset by squab-
bling within the SSF about the extent of support due
to the ILP. Keir Hardie himself was reproved for com-
municating directly with Connolly, whom he had met
often in Edinburgh and Leith and had come to respect.
For Connolly, never patient with the parochial petti-
ness of local organisations, it was demoralising. He
began to look for work outside Edinburgh, hoping

that the reputation he had made as a speaker in township like Leith and Falkirk would help. A colleague [13]
wrote in *Justice* in June of Connolly's need of a job,
and also of his virtues: knowledge, fluency, untiring
zeal, and a good strong voice ideal for outdoor meetings. No solid offers of work resulted, and Connolly
had time in the next few months to build up the prestige of the SSF. He arranged a series of public lectures
in the autumn and winter of 1895—96, delivered by
an assortment of socialist luminaries, including Edward
Aveling of the Socialist League, Henry Hyndman of
the SDF, and George Lansbury, the future leader of
the Labour Party.

Even the thrill of meeting the great names of the
left could not keep Connolly in Edinburgh, for he
was close to destitution. John Leslie was appalled to
find him contemplating emigration to Chile and wrote
a personal appeal in *Justice* — an encomium by a man
big enough to see greatness in another:

> Very few men have I met deserving of greater love
> and respect than James Connolly. I know something of Socialist propaganda . . . and I also know
> the movement in Edinburgh to its centre, and I say
> that no man has done more for the movement than
> Connolly, if they have done as much. Certainly
> nobody dared one half what he has dared in the
> assertion of his principles. Of his ability I need
> only say, as one who has had some opportunity of
> judging, he is the most able propagandist in every
> sense of the word that Scotland has turned out. . . .
> Leaving the Edinburgh Socialists to digest the matter, is there no comrade in Glasgow, Dundee, or
> anywhere else who could secure a situation for one
> of the best and most self-sacrificing men in the
> movement?

A response came from an unlikely and — to Con-

nolly — an attractive source: the Dublin Socialist Club
[14] invited him to become its paid organiser at a salary of
£1 a week. In May 1896 a subscription raised by
Edinburgh friends paid his passage to Dublin with his
wife and three daughters. He had few possessions to
transport — mainly his little library.

The Edinburgh socialists lost their driving force
and suffered for it over the next few years; their Dublin comrades were about to get more than they had
bargained for.

2
Intolerance

1

On the strength of the promised £1 a week Connolly
rented one room in a tenement in Charlemont Street.
Conditions there came as a shock to the family. The
Edinburgh slums had been bad enough, but worse
were the stench and the filth of the Dublin equivalent:
disease was commonplace, infant mortality in Dublin
the highest in the British Isles, and drunkenness and
prostitution were rife. For Lillie it was the beginning
of a period of hardship; she said later that her days in
Edinburgh had been the happiest of her life. That she
and her children remained devoted to Connolly says
much for his capacity to inspire love and loyalty, for
they were sacrificed throughout to his commitment
and idealism. He was well aware of the demands his
way of life made on them — long periods of grinding
poverty, abuse from those who thought him a dangerous fanatic, and, perhaps worst of all for a united
family, frequent and prolonged separations. Yet,
simple though she was, Lillie seems to have understood him well; she reassured him when he berated
himself for the trials he was bringing on them all, and,
grateful for his warmth, strength and fidelity, and
respectful of his integrity, she is never known to have
expressed resentment.

The first few months in Dublin were particularly
hard for the family, for even the £1 a week was rarely
forthcoming. The socialists just did not have the
money, and Connolly had no regular source of income

until he found a labouring job in September. True to
[16] form, however, he was hard at work for the cause
from the time of his arrival.

It was not easy for him to come to terms with the
priorities of the Irish socialists. Hitherto, although he
had campaigned among Irish emigrants, he had been
able to give socialism absolute precedence over
nationalism. The Dublin group had now recruited him
to mount a campaign linking Marxist thinking to the
Irish situation. The demand for separation from
Britain must underpin any socialist programme they
developed.

Connolly, though ever a man of decided views,
found the task he faced in Dublin important and
challenging enough to merit some flexibility, even
compromise, in his doctrine. The tiny Dublin Socialist
Club had great need of a man with his ability to ex-
pound, adapt and explain socialism and to galvanise
the politically inert proletariat. Although it had existed
in one form or another for fifty years, it had, during
Parnell's recent heyday, been concerned almost exclu-
sively with local union affairs, as the nationalist and
land campaigns had become the bailiwick of the parliamentary party and its supporting organisations.
Until the 1890s Marxist ideology was little known,
and it was not all plain sailing afterwards.

From the socialist point of view, it was catastrophic
that so much of the energy released from the Irish
Parliamentary Party went straight into the Gaelic
League (founded in 1893) and allied cultural organisations. They were primarily middle-class in composition and held little attraction for the workers. Seán
O'Casey, writing about his unsuccessful attempts
some years later to persuade his fellow-labourers to
join the Gaelic League, recognised that their lack of
enthusiasm was rooted in common sense:

What would the nicely-suited, white-collared res- [17]
pectable members of the refined Gaelic League do
if they found themselves in the company of these
men?[4]

The growing union movement was a more natural
home for them. Irish labour was not well organised,
mainly because there was so little heavy industry outside the north-east. Nevertheless, there was a sprinkling
of independent craft unions in Ireland and a fair
number of branches of British unions in the industrial
areas. From the late 1860s they had operated mainly
under the auspices of the British Trades Union Congress, but by the early 1890s dissatisfaction with the
force of their representation had led them to set up
their own independent congress. Keir Hardie, who
attended the inaugural meeting of the Irish Trades
Union Congress (ITUC) in 1894, saw the possibilities
of building on the general disillusion with the dis-
united Irish Party and, as Connolly had advised him,
returned to Ireland later that year to drum up support for the ILP, hoping that a strong labour movement in Ireland would influence the Irish in Britain
to vote Labour rather than Liberal. Although the ILP
had initial success in attracting recruits, by the time
of Connolly's arrival in Dublin it had lost most of the
ground gained in 1894 and 1895.

His first concern was to sell his vision of the future
to the small group that had hired him. A contemporary
described how he 'pulverised' the leaders in debate,
'shattered their little organisation, and from the frag-
ments he founded a small Irish Socialist Republican
Party' (ISRP).[5] Connolly's account of it was more
bland:

The ISRP was founded in Dublin by a few working
men whom the writer had succeeded in interesting

in his proposition that the two currents of revolutionary thought in Ireland, the socialist and the national, were not antagonistic but complementary ... that the Irish question was at bottom an economic question, and that the economic struggle must first be able to function nationally before it could function internationally, and as socialists were opposed to all oppression, so should they ever be foremost in the daily battle against all its manifestations, social and political.

The first meeting was held on 29 May 1896, when the eight men present agreed to the establishment of the ISRP and appointed Connolly secretary. A week later he was the main speaking attraction at the first of a weekly series of public meetings at the Custom House. His accent infuriated some. At one meeting a barrage of cabbage-stalks accompanied shouts of 'You're not an Irishman!' Less publicly, Connolly organised educational meetings for the handful of recruits and by September had written and printed the ISRP manifesto, which owed a great deal to the democratic—reformist approach of the British SDF. The party's aims included 'public ownership by the Irish people of the land and instruments of production, distribution and exchange'. Aims for socialist politicians included nationalisation of railways and canals; the establishment of state banks issuing loans at cost; a graduated income tax; state pensions for the aged, infirm, widows and orphans; free maintenance for children; a forty-eight-hour working week; a minimum wage; extension of public ownership; free education; and universal suffrage. It called also for the establishment of an Irish republic 'and the subsequent conversion of the means of production, distribution and exchange into the common property of society, to be held and controlled by a democratic state in the interest of the entire community'. Preceding the details of the manifesto was the Desmoulins aphorism [19] 'The great appear great because we are on our knees: let us rise' which Connolly had read in the *Labour Chronicle* two years earlier and which he was to quote frequently during the rest of his life.

The very concept of an Irish socialist republic was novel. Connolly's justification for the ISRP was developed at some length in three articles in the *Labour Leader* the month after publication of the manifesto. Entitled 'Ireland for the Irish', they were designed to persuade the journal's largely British readership that the establishment of an Irish republic was a necessary prerequisite for the achievement of a socialist society. This was against the grain of British Marxist orthodoxy, which favoured Home Rule for Ireland as a necessary 'liberal' step which must historically precede a general working-class takeover throughout the British Empire. Connolly briefly surveyed two centuries of Irish history in an effort to prove that current Irish Parliamentary Party aims were both inadequate and inappropriate to the true needs of Ireland. Until the seventeenth century, he argued, when the system was smashed by the English government, a pattern of common ownership of land had existed — a pattern integral to the Irish way of life. It was a plea for flexibility in applying Marxist historical determinism to Ireland. Those who believed that all societies had to go through pre-determined stages — 'communism, chattel slavery, feudalism and wage-slavery' — before achieving a just system might see the persistence for so long in Ireland of clan ownership as evidence of 'retarded economical [*sic*] development'.

But the sympathetic student of history, who believed in the possibility of a people by political intuition anticipating the lessons afterwards revealed to them in the sad school of experience, will not be indisposed to join with the ardent Irish patriot in his lavish expressions of admiration for the sagacity of his Celtic forefathers, who foreshadowed in the democratic organisation of the Irish clan the more perfect organisation of the free society of the future.

According to Connolly's analysis, the English had destroyed this primitive communism, installing their own system of private ownership. The bourgeois-dominated Irish political nationalists were beneficiaries, and sought merely to extend ownership to Irish tenants – a development that would only perpetuate the injustice inherent in any form of land ownership 'since it would leave out of account the entire labouring class as well as the dispossessed millions of former tenants who[m] landlord rule had driven into the Irish towns or across the seas'. In any case, it would be unworkable, as it offered no means of large-scale modernisation of agriculture; only land nationalisation could achieve that. Home Rule, overlaid on an alien economic system, would be an historical irrelevance in Marxist terms.

He anticipated that his panacea for the economic and social evils of Ireland – an Irish socialist republic – would engender hostility among the internationalists, who saw nationalism as a bar to world-wide socialist progress.

The interests of labor all the world over are identical, it is true, but it is also true that each country had better work out its own salvation on the lines most congenial to its own people.

And for Ireland, he maintained, salvation lay in the adoption of the republican and reformist programme of the ISRP.

Connolly showed, in these brave and incisive articles, a confidence bred of his thorough grounding in scientific socialism and a breadth of mind which allowed him to use it as a tool, not serve it as a master. His arguments were powerfully made, if perhaps founded on an unduly romantic understanding of clan ownership and a certain ignorance of the strength of rural Ireland's land hunger. In their use of the Gaelic tradition they were an impressive start to his work of hibernicising Marxism, as Mao Tse-tung was to sinify it.

Such was Connolly's greatest achievement, for virtually no one had applied radical ideas of such system and extremism to the Irish land or national questions for generations. For all the rapid progress he was making intellectually, however, there was small hope yet of seeing his ideas through in any practical way. Recruitment into the ISRP from the mainstream of radical nationalists in Ireland was essential, and it was to this that he devoted his energies from the beginning of 1897.

2

Connolly had already established links with the *Shan Van Vocht*, a republican journal edited from Belfast by Alice Milligan. It reviewed favourably his first pamphlet, a selection of the writings of James Fintan Lalor, one of the 1848 revolutionaries, who had argued for the common ownership of Irish land. He also contributed to the journal in November 1896 an article entitled 'Can Irish Republicans be Politicians?'. The answer was yes; Connolly argued against insurrection without the sanction of the people and urged nationalists to support only a political party seeking democratic support for a republic. He denounced those who promoted physical force, divorced from a common objective, as the only test of advanced nationalism. The true criterion was an individual's or a party's commitment to the creation of a socialist state.

In January 1897, as a plethora of committees were planning commemorations of the 1798 rebellion, he contributed to the *Shan Van Vocht* an article, 'Nationalism and Socialism', on the limitations of tradition. In this he argued that devotion to a heritage should not outweigh determination to solve the problems of the present and future, lest nationalists finu themselves led 'into a worship of the past, or [the] crystallising [of] nationalism into a tradition — glorious and heroic indeed, but still only a tradition'. Without a programme there was no point in commemoration. True nationalists should declare themselves for a republic — even at the expense of middle-class support.

Despite ideological reservations, Alice Milligan was impressed with Connolly's argument. She asked her young brother, Ernest, to visit him in Dublin, where he was promptly recruited into the ISRP. Returning to set up a tiny branch of the ISRP in Belfast, Milligan reported Connolly to be 'terribly earnest in conversation', but with a rich sense of humour. It was a common response. (In Dublin the chief ISRP stalwarts included Tom, Jack and Murtagh Lyng and Thomas, Daniel and, from 1899, William O'Brien. Recruitment was slow; attendance at private meetings rarely exceeded fifteen. Their enthusiasm, and Connolly's formidable leadership, compensated for lack of numbers, even if they sometimes resented his dogmatism and aggression.)

Connolly's public scepticism about the commemoration movement had rendered the ISRP unwelcome in the mainstream, so he founded the 'Rank and File '98 Club' to disseminate his own interpretation of 1798: the leaders, particularly Wolfe Tone, had fought for a socialist republic, as was

shown by extracts from their writings published by
Connolly and financed by a loan from the O'Briens' [23]
mother.

The high spot of 1897 for the ISRP was its counter-
demonstration against the celebrations of Queen
Victoria's Diamond Jubilee in June. Connolly had the
support of Maud Gonne, a romantic — and somewhat
histrionic — nationalist. She came to know and respect Connolly early in 1897 and accepted his invitation to address an ISRP anti-Jubilee meeting. Although
she felt great compassion for the poor, she was upset
to find herself billed as the main attraction at a socialist meeting. Yeats, Maud's worshipper, was present
when she told Connolly she was withdrawing, and his
heart was touched by 'the young man and his look of
melancholy'.[6] He persuaded her to reconsider. Maud
visited the family tenement and was so appalled by
the poverty she found there (there was a new baby,
Ina) that she changed her mind again.

They were natural allies, sharing a penchant for the
bold move and the flamboyant gesture. For the main
anti-Jubilee protest Maud provided black flags (the
symbol of the unemployed) embroidered with statis-
tics of famine deaths and evictions, and secured a
window in the city from which lantern slides of evic-
tion scenes and Irish patriots imprisoned or executed
during Victoria's reign could be thrown onto a large
screen. On Jubilee Day she and Yeats joined a procession led by a workers' band and an ISRP member
pushing a cart draped in black flags on which rested
a black coffin inscribed 'British Empire'. As the procession grew and windows began to be smashed, the
police started to make baton charges. The procession
was stopped at O'Connell Bridge, and rather than
have the coffin confiscated Connolly ordered it to
be tossed into the Liffey. He was imprisoned overnight until Maud paid his fine. Later in the evening

her magic lantern show was a huge success, but in
[24] the fighting with the police an old woman was killed.
The bloody Dublin demonstration, along with others
in Cork and Limerick, gained a great deal of press
attention.

The ISRP did not rest on their laurels. Two months
later, to coincide with a visit by the Duke and Duchess
of York, they held a meeting to commemorate the
landing of the French at Killala in 1798. It was broken
up by police, as was an ISRP meeting on the following Sunday.

Connolly did not rely on such local exploits to win
the allegiance of advanced nationalists. He initiated a
controversy by contributing to the *Shan Van Vocht*
an article proposing a political party to take the socialist and republican struggle into Westminster. Alice
Milligan abhorred the idea: it would mean taking the
oath of allegiance at Westminster. Connolly, eternally
pragmatic, argued against leaving the anti-separatist,
pro-monarchical MPs unchallenged at the seat of
government, but he made little headway with the
majority of republicans and found himself under
attack from Edinburgh internationalists too. In the
Labour Leader the ISRP was denounced as a chauvin-
ist organisation. Connolly fought back strongly,
claiming the right under socialism of every nation to
decide its own destiny. Orthodox British socialism
was wrong; the Home Rulers should not be praised as
more internationalist than the republicans simply
because they shunned separatism. They were a class
enemy, wishing to reproduce in Ireland 'all the political and social manifestations which accompany
capitalist supremacy in Great Britain'.

In the *Labour Leader* Connolly, undeterred by
criticism, claimed great progress for the ISRP in only
eighteen months. Its influence had spread to remote
parts of the country, and even as far as the United

States, where its appeal to Irish-Americans to support the Socialist Labour Party (SLP) of America had been incorporated in 60,000 copies of a leaflet issued by that organisation. Connolly was inspired to offer Irishmen abroad associate membership of the ISRP. The SLP's *Weekly People* invited Connolly to cover the famine in Mayo and Kerry. He had already co-operated with Maud Gonne in the preparation of a manifesto, *The Rights of Life and the Rights of Property*, which urged the prevention of a repetition of the Great Famine of 1847—48. Tenants should refuse to pay rent or allow the export of food while Irish people went hungry at home. Maud provided the £25 printing costs. They drew on the writings of fathers of the Irish Church to justify such actions:

The very highest authorities on the doctrine of the church agree that no *human* law can stand between starving people and their right to food, including their right to take that food whenever they find it, openly or secretly, with or without the owner's permission.

While Maud led successful agitations in Mayo, Connolly found in Kerry that relief workers, including many clergy, had already put the needs of the victims before the rights of property, and measures were far more effective than fifty years earlier.

Nevertheless, Connolly was deeply moved by the misery in Kerry, the blame for which, in his *Weekly People* articles, he attributed not so much to foreign government or landlordism as to the failure of the system of small farming. What he had seen reinforced the belief — stated in a pamphlet, *Erin's Hope* (a thematic selection from his 1896 writings) — that in modern conditions the small farmer was doomed to economic failure, be he tenant or proprietor.

If Connolly had hoped that the 1798 commemoration would provide him with further opportunities for dramatic public gestures, he was to be disappointed. The Home Rulers had become involved, and Connolly disaffiliated his '98 Club from the main movement. For a time the club met after ISRP meetings, mainly for the singing of patriotic songs, and Connolly made an oration at the grave of Wolfe Tone. These activities created little stir; Maud Gonne had stayed with the main commemoration group during the crucial planning stage, although she too eventually walked out in disgust.

The ISRP moved away for a time from the specifically anti-imperialist demonstrations of 1897 and adopted again the broader educational approach. Lectures and public meetings considered the impact of socialism on such issues as disarmament, price rises, old-age pensions, the temperance movement and trade unionism. There had been a marked shift in Connolly's attitude to this last issue. In Edinburgh the orthodox socialist view (which he shared) was that trade unions shored up the capitalist structure and were a useless instrument for socialist advance. The third volume of Marx's *Capital* (published in 1894) argued strongly for worker co-operation which would in time lead, in the post-capitalist state, to worker control of industry. Connolly accepted the point and in 1898 welcomed the sponsoring of election candidates by Dublin trade unions.

Connolly drove himself relentlessly through endless disappointments and frustrations. Money was short, as always. Either he was unemployed and dependent on whatever few shillings the ISRP could provide, or, when he did have work, he was trying to combine his socialist mission with hard physical labour. He and Lillie had another daughter, Máire, and simply feeding the family was a constant worry. The purchase of clothes and boots for the manual job he had found in September 1896 had forced them to pawn all but the bare necessities. Increasingly, potential employers were deterred by his growing political notoriety.

He was stubborn. Although the growing unity of the Home Rule movement limited expansion of his group, he decided to launch an ISRP paper as a platform for his own gospel and, perhaps, a source of a living wage. In July 1898 he went to Scotland to seek financial help for the forthcoming *Workers' Republic*. Such was the respect he still enjoyed there that he soon had enough capital to start the venture. Keir Hardie himself lent £50.

A 'literary champion of Irish Democracy', the weekly would advocate 'an Irish Republic, the abolition of landlordism, wage-slavery, the co-operative organisation of industry under Irish representative governing bodies'. The first issue appeared on 14 August 1898, a date chosen to coincide with the foundation-stone ceremony at the official '98 memorial. It vigorously assailed the leadership for alleging that the men of 1798, the United Irishmen, had been a 'union of class and creed'. What, it demanded to know, was the 'feasibility of uniting in one movement underpaid labourers and overpaid masters'? Tone's principles 'could only be realised in a socialist republic'. Connolly was, of course, doing the same job on the 1798 leaders — though from a different vantage-point — as were the Home Rulers. Just as they were marshalling the martyrs behind the Home Rule banner, so Connolly was mobilising them in the class war. He never shifted his view that the social revolution must come about through the masses and the masses alone. The Land League (of 1879—81), in living memory, was a model of what an awakened class-consciousness could [28] achieve. Connolly the worker might regard Maud Gonne as an ally, but he always held that class unity was a myth fostered by capitalists. There was no future for landlord or capitalist in the new Ireland for which he fought; the struggle was not to unite class with class but to achieve solidarity among workers of all creeds and callings.

In the August issue he launched a bitter attack on religious sectarianism. The principle of the *Workers' Republic* was to '*unite* the workers and to bury in one common grave the religious hatreds, the provincial jealousies, and the mutual distrusts upon which oppression has so long depended for security'.

The paper survived until late October 1898; it had sold well in Dublin and Belfast for its first few weeks, but public interest declined. The old problem of reconciling socialism with republicanism contributed to its failure. There was only a very narrow common ground between a Belfast socialist and a Dublin nationalist; the newspaper's republicanism repelled the one, while the other rejected its Marxism. In October he did little to boost his circulation when he lambasted the apolitical language and culture movement – 'You cannot teach starving men Gaelic.' He had cut himself off from compromise in the very first issue:

We are Republicans because we are Socialists, and therefore enemies to all privileges; *and because we would have the Irish people complete masters of their own destinies, nationally and internationally, fully competent to work out their own salvation.*

For all his intelligence, Connolly was never given to subtlety of expression, preferring the unequivocal statement of his views. In that lay much of his strength as a Marxist interpreter; no one could ever be in any doubt about his stance. His were not the tactics to win mass support, however, and no amount of useful polemic on modern warfare and its capitalist causes, the uselessness of a peasant proprietary or the need for trade unionists as political activists was likely to win many recruits. Such articles, after all, sought to undermine the basic principles of most sections of Irish politics.

4

The failure of the *Workers' Republic* could not be permitted to slow down work in the greater cause whose flagship it had been. Connolly's ISRP held a number of open-air meetings in support of their (unsuccessful) candidate in the local government elections in Dublin. Connolly continued to run educational meetings in Dublin and gave a public lecture in Cork in February on the theme of 'Labour and Revolution', again attacking middle-class leadership in a nationalist party. His financial circumstances were no better. In March he wrote to Daniel O'Brien that he had lost a manual job he had just got: 'Having been on short commons so long, [I] am unable to perform such work when I get it.' He was receiving only 7s a week from the party, and was reluctant to take even that from comrades who could ill afford it. He asked in humiliation for the loan of £2 to buy stock to set up as a peddlar — otherwise he could not stay in Ireland.

> It would tear my heart-strings out to leave Ireland now after all my toil and privation — and unless I succeed in this instance the welfare, nay the mere necessity of feeding my family will leave me no alternative.

He did not continue long as a peddlar. He decided to start the *Workers' Republic* up again, this time print-

ing it himself on a small hand press rather than pay a
[30] commercial printer. He took a more realistic decision
this time: no new issue would appear until the last
had sold out.

Connolly was again the main contributor, and the
formula was as before. He attacked the notion that
religion and socialism were incompatible:

> Socialism, as a party, bases itself upon its knowledge
> of facts, of economic truths, and leaves the building
> up of religious ideals or faiths to the outside public,
> or to its individual members if they so will. It is
> neither Freethinker nor Christian, Turk nor Jew,
> Buddhist nor Idolator, Mahommedan nor Parsee —
> it is only HUMAN.

The battleground must be cleared

> for the final struggle between the only two parties
> possessed of a logical reason for existence — the
> Conservative party defending the strongholds of
> monarchy, aristocracy, and capitalism; and the
> Socialist party storming those strongholds in the
> interests of human freedom.

Liberalism was simply 'a buffer between the contend-
ing forces of tyranny and freedom', and its extirpation
was a priority. Its ally, the parliamentary party with
its policy of Home Rule, was 'but capitalist Liberalism, speaking with an Irish accent'.

Connolly was a natural educator, and he performed
an invaluable service to his comrades in using his more
powerful mind and wide reading (much of his spare
time when he was unemployed was spent in intensive
study in the National Library) to furnish them with
ammunition on the contentious issues of the day. In a
series of articles called 'Workshop Talks' he tackled,
in lighthearted and readable prose, the criticisms that
the socialist might meet in his workplace: that social-

ism was a foreign importation; that old-age pensions would destroy morale and character; that socialism was impractical, anti-nationalist or anti-religious. He demonstrated again and again his ability to speak to his readers on their own level, and the sardonic humour that made him good company was given free reign:

Whoop it up for liberty!
'Let us free Ireland,' says the patriot who won't touch Socialism.
Let us all join together and cr-r-rush the br-r-rutal Saxon. Let us all join together, says he, all classes and creeds.
And, says the town worker, after we have crushed the Saxon and freed Ireland, what will we do?
Oh, then you can go back to your slums, same as before. . . .
After Ireland is free, says the patriot who won't touch Socialism, we will protect all classes, and if you won't pay your rent you will be evicted same as now. But the evicting party, under command of the sheriff, will wear green uniforms and the Harp without the Crown, and the warrant turning you out on the roadside will be stamped with the arms of the Irish Republic. Now, isn't that worth fighting for?

In the second half of 1899 he was exercised by the appropriate Irish response to the Boer War — expressing the virulent anti-imperialism which was to be a crucial factor in his career. Although Britain did not declare war until October, it was clear by the summer of 1899 that conflict with the Boers was imminent. Nationalist feeling in Ireland was high and inevitably pro-Boer, against what was seen as imperialist aggression. Connolly explained in the *Workers' Republic* in

August that the war was a ploy by 'an unscrupulous [32] gang of capitalists to get into their hands the immense riches of the diamond fields'. He regretted the lack of unity among the working class which prevented them taking advantage of the transfer of British troops from Ireland to the Transvaal. The Boer crisis, like the Jubilee before it, goaded Connolly into public agitation. His old ally was available. Maud Gonne sent to an ISRP meeting on 27 August (the first public meeting to be held in Ireland in support of the Boers) a letter proposing that protest meetings be held throughout Ireland. An uncompromising resolution drafted by Connolly was adopted:

> WHEREAS the government of this country is maintained upon the bayonets of an occupying army against the will of the people;
>
> WHEREAS there were in India, Egypt and other portions of the British Empire other and much larger populations also kept down in forced subjection;
>
> WHEREAS a country that thus keeps down subject populations by the use of the hangman, the bullet or the sword, has no right to preach to another about its duties towards its population;
>
> THEREFORE BE IT RESOLVED that this meeting denounces the interference of the British capitalist government in the internal affairs of the Transvaal Republic as an act of criminal aggression, wishes long life to the Republic, and trusts that our fellow-countrymen will, if need be, take up arms in defence of their adopted country.

The ISRP was too small and too poor to make much impact. With a branch in Cork and supporters in Belfast (which branch had collapsed), Limerick, Dundalk, Waterford and Portadown, membership was in only double figures. Still, Connolly's talents and

energy made him a useful limb of the Irish Transvaal
Committee, set up by Maud Gonne and Arthur [33]
Griffith, editor of the separatist *United Irishman*.
Griffith was opposed to an armed uprising, which he
considered impractical. Instead he strove to awaken a
sense of self-respect in the nation as the first stage
in its progress towards freedom. He had no time for
Connolly's socialism, but was prepared to use his
words or his party when it suited him. The committee
organised several anti-war rallies during the autumn
of 1899, contributing to a fall in British army
recruitment.

Just before Christmas Connolly and Maud Gonne
had another opportunity for eye-catching mischief:
Trinity College was to confer an honorary degree on
Joseph Chamberlain, a Liberal turned Unionist obnox-
ious to every shade of nationalist opinion, and a
protest was planned. The main speakers were to be
Michael Davitt and William Redmond, MP, but the
British administration in Dublin Castle proscribed
the meeting. The only speakers to assemble in Abbey
Street were Connolly, Maud, the veteran Fenian John
O'Leary, and Pat O'Brien, MP, deputising for Davitt.
They set off in a wagon, but the driver refused a
police instruction to turn back and was hauled away.
Connolly seized the reins and drove at a gallop through
the police cordon to Beresford Place, where a large
crowd shouted approval as Maud read out the resolution supporting the Boers. The police dispersed the
onlookers and led the wagon into a nearby barracks,
but the presence of an MP among those detained
ensured their quick release. Unable to return to Beresford Place, they drove along Abbey Street across
Sackville Street (later O'Connell Street). Seán O'Casey
watched from the crowd:

A stout, short, stocky man, whose face was hidden

by a wide-awake hat, was driving them ... and with them was a young woman with long lovely yellow hair, smiling happily, like a child out on her first excursion.

Maud recalled later that as they raced by Dublin Castle Connolly turned and asked if he should seize the Castle, where only two sentries stood on duty. Their escapade over, they repaired more soberly to Foster Place, where ISRP meetings were held, only to have yet another meeting broken up. Connolly's elation at having thumbed his nose again at the British Empire was dampened when he discovered the consequences: his little hand press had been smashed in a police raid, and the *Workers' Republic* was again out of business.

5

The omens for socialist advance were bleak early in 1900. The ISRP candidate in the January municipal elections, like Labour candidates throughout the country, was heavily defeated. The Irish parliamentarians, after a decade of internecine strife, were united again under the leadership of John Redmond. Although the pro-Boer protests continued successfully, they did little to spread the ISRP's distinctive philosophy since the Transvaal Committee represented the whole spread of nationalist opinion. Connolly was one of the many incensed by the visit to Ireland, in April 1900, of Queen Victoria, sent over in her eighty-first year to try to undo the damage to the recruitment figures. In a demonstration against her presence both Connolly and Griffith were injured by police batons. Not that there was much need for violent protest against the Queen's visit; the immense efforts of the Dublin administration to rouse the populace to enthusiasm earned only a pregnant silence from the crowds lining her route. Connolly had played his part with a manifesto declaring monarchy to be 'a survival of the tyranny imposed by the hand of greed and treachery in the darkest and most ignorant days of our history', but he had to miss most of the Queen's month-long visit. His father was dying in Edinburgh, and Connolly went to him.

Returning to Dublin in May, he revived the *Workers' Republic* and protested vehemently against the mounting attacks on civil liberties. The *United Irishman's* issue of 17 April had been suppressed because of a contribution from Maud Gonne entitled 'The Famine Queen', and, though no admirer of Griffith, Connolly denounced such denials of press freedom and organised protest meetings against police coercion. Yet as the parliamentary party united on the one hand, and Griffith, the champion of passive resistance, gained ground on the other, the ISRP remained a small voice crying on the fringes of Irish political life. Connolly wrote enthusiastically in July 1900 about Maud Gonne's Patriotic Children's Treat, a reward to those who had boycotted the Queen's celebrations, but he cannot have been blind to the fact that its attendance by 30,000 children was a triumph for Maud, her new organisation — Inghinidhe na hÉireann (Daughters of Erin) — and her political mentor, Griffith, and marked the emergence of a political force which would serve only to block any ISRP advances. The occasion did, however, evoke from him a memorable declaration of priorities, in sharp contrast with the sentimental declarations of love for the motherland to which romantic nationalists were fashionably given:

Ireland without her people is nothing to me, and the man who is bubbling over with love and enthusiasm for 'Ireland', and can yet pass unmoved through our streets and witness all the wrong and the suffering, the shame and the degradation wrought on the people of Ireland, aye, wrought by Irishmen upon Irishmen and women, without burning to end it, is, in my opinion, a fraud and a liar in his heart, no matter how he loves that combination of chemical elements which he is pleased to call 'Ireland'.

Though weak at home, the ISRP stepped briefly on to the international stage, sending two delegates to the International Socialist Congress in Paris. Even Griffith was impressed by this recognition of Irish nationhood, although the delegates received scant sympathy for their policy of independence from Britain. In a battle over the French socialist deputy, Millerand, only the Irish and Bulgarian delegations voted uncompromisingly to censure him for joining a non-socialist government. Another delegate, Karl Kautsky, had tabled a compromise resolution, but, together with the extreme left, the ISRP line was that Millerand's action was 'an international scandal'. Mutual support stopped there. Rosa Luxemburg, the Polish-born German socialist leader, attacked the 'nationalist heresy' inherent in dreams of reuniting Poland. To her, and to many within the socialist movement, independence movements were a dangerous obstacle to the achievement of international socialist revolution. This was a criticism that Connolly met often from British socialists and which he was never able to counter successfully.

He had in any case already lost friends in Britain. His pro-Boer activities had alienated some; his anti-Home Rule propaganda alienated more. In March a Fabian lecturer, Bruce Glasier, in an article in *Clarion*, described him patronisingly, though not wholly unsympathetically, participating in an anti-war demonstration: 'How I envied him his self-indulgence and irresponsibility. How straight and broad, but ah! how exhilarating seemed the path along which he was careering with the policemen at his heels.' Connolly counter-attacked furiously in the columns of *Justice*, denouncing the bourgeois Fabians, whose support for the war against the Boers appalled him. He had a breach too with the ILP, many of whom, like Keir Hardie, appalled at the poor showing of Labour in Irish elections, were seeking to strengthen their appeal to Irish emigrants in Britain by expressing support for Home Rule. Not surprisingly, relations between Hardie and Connolly grew cooler, although Connolly's gratitude for past help never permitted any hostility.

In the spring of 1901 Connolly decided to seek speaking engagements in Britain. He had pressing financial reasons for doing so. (The previous Christmas he had brought home two shillings of ISRP money. In February Lillie had given birth to their sixth child, Roderick. The *Workers' Republic* was staggering on from crisis to crisis. After collapsing in the summer of 1900 it had been revived for the fourth time in October, but both the party's and Connolly's future prospects were bleak.) He was also anxious to take his various disagreements with British socialists into their own camp.

The ISRP's leftist stance on the Kautsky resolution made Connolly *persona non grata* in many SDF branches, but he was welcome in Scotland and some parts of England. During May and June he spoke in Glasgow, Falkirk, Aberdeen and Leith. One of his hearers wrote of him:

He possesses an attribute comparatively rare among socialist lecturers, that of being at the same time simple and perfectly intelligible to the ordinary man, and also perfectly accurate and rigid in his adherence to scientific verity.[7]

The first part of that judgment at least was unchallengeable. He proved so successful in arousing interest on a week-long propaganda campaign in Salford that he was asked to return there again in September and October, by which time the town boasted (though not for long) a branch of the ISRP, set up by Irish emigrant miners. In his address to their first public meeting Connolly made a clear distinction between the two main streams of the SDF – now described in terms imported from the US as 'fakirs' and 'clear-cuts'. Where the fakirs, or reformists, favoured the Kautsky resolution and the Home Rule movement, the clear-cuts should believe, in Connolly's words, that socialism should 'accept no government position which it cannot conquer through its own strength at the ballot-box'. They should follow the ISRP line on Ireland. A future Labour MP described him as 'one of the most convincing speakers I ever heard in my life, a man with a great passion for the cause of the labouring classes, and probably a greater passion for the cause of Ireland'. Following his Salford triumphs, he spoke to sizeable audiences in Reading, where he gained no recruits, to noisy meetings in Oxford (where during one *fracas* he is alleged to have knocked out four troublemakers with a flag-pole) and with some minor success in North London. His distrust of capitalist reforms was expressed thus: 'If the workers ask for the capitalist baker's shop, he will throw the loaves at them to keep them out.'

The tour was not an overwhelming success, but it augmented his reputation as a propagandist and provided a welcome boost for his party's funds. He had been back and forth to Dublin during the summer and corresponded with colleagues there. Murtagh Lyng wrote to ask if he were interested in organising a union for the tram-car workers. Connolly turned the idea down and went on to chastise ISRP members for failing to conduct enough open-air meetings. He drew the injured response that he was not taking enough account of their difficulties and, by being 'much too *vitriolic*' in his remarks, was demotivating his friends. That warning did not deter Connolly, who could never forgive any slackening of effort, from complaining about a delay in the publication of the *Workers' Republic*. However, good news of ISRP activities brought congratulations:

There were so many evil prophets in Dublin saying that the movement would go slump if I left Dublin that your progress since I left has been doubly gratifying to me — proving that the ISRP was well able to stand on its own feet, and that its growth depended upon correct principles and not upon one's personality. If all those who can work for Socialism in Ireland would work I might content myself in exile, and never would be missed, which would be a greater tribute to my work of the past five years than if my presence was indispensable.

When he returned to Dublin in mid-October the United Labourers had elected him to the Dublin Trades Council, and he was nominated in November as Labour candidate for the Wood Quay ward in the council elections. He lost by a heavy majority in the January 1902 election, after a campaign in which he was pilloried as anti-Catholic.

The *Workers' Republic* was again suspended for a few months, but reappeared in March from a new printing machine, on which also was produced an ISRP appeal to British socialists to oppose the Irish Parliamentary Party. The latter piece was reprinted in Germany, France and in the American SLP's *Weekly People*.

6

Connolly was by now strongly under the influence of the SLP leader, Daniel De Leon, whose party exchanged propaganda with the ISRP and helped it financially. De Leon was intellectual, rigidly doctrinaire and uncompromising; he believed that a socialist party should be as 'intolerant as science'. Any alliance with organisations not themselves ideologically pure was corruption, indirectly bolstering up capitalist institutions; reformist attempts to alleviate the workers' lot merely gave credibility to the bourgeois state. Orthodox trade unions, organised along craft lines, came under attack in his *What Means This Strike?* (published in 1898) for their divisiveness. De Leon had been strongly influenced by the syndicalist (or industrial unionist — the term Connolly preferred) 'one big union' movement which appeared throughout the English-speaking world during the first decade of the twentieth century, having emanated from France during the 1890s. In its purest form syndicalism ignored elections. Workers should seize control of the state by seizing control of its industries. De Leon's view was different. He proposed what he called 'dual unionism', which required that socialist industrial unions be set up, as rivals to the existing craft unions, subordinate to the machine of an ideologically pure party having no truck with reformist or compromising heresies. Connolly knew too much of human misery to go all the way with De Leon's condemnation of social reforms, but had gradually accepted most of his views. In his revision in 1902 of *Erin's Hope* for publication in America he showed a distinct switch from social democratic reformism to the hardline De Leonist sectarianism — 'No revolutionists can safely invite the co-operation of men or classes whose ideals are not theirs and whom, therefore, they may be compelled to fight at some future critical stage.' It was under the influence of De Leon that ISRP members had taken their uncompromising stance at the Paris International Socialist Congress.

Once spring came and evening meetings were again possible, Connolly went back to propaganda work in Scotland and England. He had been invited to America by the SLP and was hoping that with the help of the SLP, the United Labourers of Ireland and ISRP fund-raising efforts, enough money might be found to make the trip possible. While he waited he found himself embroiled in disputes within the SDF, many of whom, particularly in Scotland, were also under De Leonist influence. Connolly had been the chief scourge of the SDF's reformist leadership over the Kautsky resolution; it was inevitable that he should throw in his lot with the Scots dissenters. He agreed that the ISRP press should publish for them a monthly called *The Socialist* which would contain much editorial material in common with the *Workers' Republic*. The editor of *The Socialist*, J. Carstairs Matheson, became a friend and correspondent.

Connolly toured Scotland and England preaching the doctrines of the now ideologically pure ISRP. (He did not always stick to the same old subjects. One of his addresses analysed the growth of industrial trusts, using them as evidence that competition was unnecessary in industry: the workers' priority should not be to oppose such trusts but to capture the political power necessary to use all productive property for the good of the human race.) Although away for long periods, he did not ignore Dublin, but kept up a stream of letters urging comrades to be more efficient in getting the *Workers' Republic* out, emphasising the need for further recruitment, criticising the shortcomings of Cork ISRP members and discussing arrangements for financing his American trip. Although his letters tended to be businesslike, there are occasional human passages. In a letter to William O'Brien he described the humiliation he had suffered in waiting five months for a suit to be completed:

> I had to approach the parties concerned so often and vainly until I felt like a beggar — all this combined to so humiliate me and outrage my self-respect that it at one time nearly, indeed actually, made me resolve never to go back to Dublin again. But having once put my hand to the plow I cannot turn back, and as a matter of fact the movement in Ireland, and Ireland itself, is so twined up in my very existence that I could not abandon it even if I would.[8]

Temporary abandonment was imminent, though. After returning in August to spend a few days with his family, Connolly sailed to the United States for a five-month tour.

3
Charity

1

De Leon had great hopes for Connolly. He liked admirers, and Connolly's prominence in Britain and Ireland as an exponent of De Leonism had been taken note of. De Leon, a man of powerful intellect, energy and commitment, was a giant of the American socialist movement. He saw Connolly's potential usefulness as twofold: he could win Irish-American recruits for the SLP while in the country and return across the Atlantic more strongly evangelist than before.

In a crowded tour Connolly had little time to get involved in the internal politics of the SLP, whose reception of him was dazzling. At the first meeting in New York on 15 September 1902, held to introduce him to the party as well as inaugurate the SLP state campaign in the Congressional elections, he admitted to feeling at a disadvantage before such a large gathering: 'Though accustomed to addressing audiences of the working class in England, Scotland and my own country, I never stood before such a crowd before.' To what the *Weekly People* described as 'tumultuous applause', Connolly (whom the paper termed a 'sturdy Irish proletarian') was dispatched on his mission of persuading the Irish emigrants to forget the prejudices of a lifetime, turn their backs on the Home Rule movement and vote for the SLP.

The tour was moderately successful, bringing in an appreciable number of subscriptions for the *Workers' Republic,* and at least bringing the SLP to the serious

attention of large numbers of Irish-Americans. Sleep-
[44] ing almost every night in a new town, he spoke at
meetings as far west as California and as far north as
Canada. It was a gruelling tour, for although he was
paid enough to keep him on the road and his family
at home, he could afford few comforts and was generally reliant on whatever local hospitality the poor
communities he visited could provide. He was alienated
by the United States. Although he granted its greater
affluence, he condemned American egotism and the
widespread lawbreaking, which he attributed to an
excess of individualism. Still, the experience was
an exhilarating one, culminating in a large farewell
meeting in New York on 2 January 1903, where
De Leon gave the valedictory address.

Connolly had worries about the ISRP while in
America. He had collected enough subscriptions to
keep his paper afloat for a long time and was appalled
to find that his comrades at home were being remiss
about publishing it. In November a furious letter to
Daniel O'Brien demanded an explanation, boding ill
for the future unity of the ISRP:

> Here am I, knocking life out of myself . . . telling
> everybody that the paper will appear more regularly
> in the future than in the past, and you people at
> home have not the common manliness to try and
> stand by my work by getting out the paper as
> promised. You may think it all a joke, but I think
> that you all ought to be damned well ashamed of
> yourselves. . . . I am ashamed, heartily ashamed of
> the whole gang of you. If some of you do not
> think the cause of the Socialist Republic worth
> working for, why in Heaven's name do you not
> get out of the Party? We would be better starting
> again with half a dozen men as before than be
> cumbered by the presence of a crowd who are

only Socialists because it gives them the reputation for originality.

He had always been testy, quick to take offence and prone to bully rather than cajole. As he admitted himself, 'I have such an unfortunate knack, as you know, of saying things that turn my best friends into enemies.'[9] The increased self-confidence gained from his tour was hardly likely to make him any more circumspect. On his return, discord was immediate. He had already complained from America at the feeble preparations for the January municipal elections, and he was now disappointed (running this time on a purely socialist, non-republican ticket) to secure only about half his previous vote in the same Wood Quay ward. His reservations about his colleagues' commitment turned to fury when he discovered what had been happening in the ISRP itself. In the previous year a licensed bar had been set up on party premises while Connolly was in Britain, and during his absence in America it had proved highly popular with the members. Himself meticulous about organisation (regular minutes of meetings had been kept from the outset; accounts had been audited), he had too great a sense of mission to comprehend, let alone tolerate, the fallibility of his fellows. Not that he did not have excellent grounds for complaint: the bar had been badly managed, and its losses made good from American subscriptions to the *Workers' Republic*. What Matheson described as his 'confoundedly disagreeable integrity and incorruptibility'[10] was outraged but his attempt to have the committee dismissed backfired. The party refused to pay a bill to avoid foreclosure on the printing press, and on 18 February he tendered his resignation in protest. To his chagrin it was accepted. Some ISRP members had been chafing under Connolly for a long time. No sooner had they

swallowed his brand of social democracy than he was
[46] force-feeding them with the rigid doctrines of De Leon.
He was invulnerable in debate, and so resentment at
his intellectual tyranny erupted over a relatively trivial
matter.

He soon rejoined the party, but irreparable damage
had been done. The ISRP had split, and several leading
members like Tom Lyng and William O'Brien had left.
By March he was pleading with Matheson to help
find him a job:

> As to work I would 'prefer', well, Chancellor of
> the Exchequer would do. But I have been a proof-
> reader, a tilelayer (ten years ago); a while you wait
> shoemaker, a mason's labourer and a carter. It is
> so long since I did hard manual labour that I feel
> queer at the thoughts of it.

April found him regretting the job offers he had turned
down in America. He was penniless. 'I consider', he
wrote to Matheson, 'that the party here has no longer
that exclusive demand on my life which led me in the
past to sacrifice my children's welfare for years in
order to build it up.' His bitterness (he described
some opponents as 'reptiles')[11] and sense of personal
hurt was lasting; in August he wrote from Scotland to
William O'Brien (for whom he always had respect)
condemning his

> quondam comrades, whose willingness to believe
> ill of me, and to wreck my work, seems to have
> grown in proportion to the extent I was successful
> in serving them. . . .
>
> My career has been unique in many things. In
> this last it is so also. Men have been driven out of
> Ireland by the British Government, and by the
> landlords, but I am the first driven forth by the
> 'Socialists'?

In the spring of 1903, while working for the Scottish District Council of the SDF, he was em- broiled in another internal row. Connolly had encouraged a new organisation in Scotland on the lines of the American SLP. He continued his attacks on the compromising character of the SDF leadership, and when the Scottish Council announced its breakaway from the SDF Connolly was behind its new manifesto. At his urging it was dubbed the Socialist Labour Party, and from late April he became its paid organiser on a three-month contract.

He made speeches, wrote proletarian songs and ran classes for prospective activists, fulfilling De Leon's hopes. Owing to the hopeless state of confusion and disarray into which the ISRP organisation in Dublin had fallen, the *Workers' Republic* was again suspended. *The Socialist* was now printed in Scotland, and Connolly had the rump of the ISRP arrange its distribution to American subscribers in lieu of the Irish paper.

The Scottish SLP never really got off the ground, and in July Connolly was forced to face the fact that it could not offer him a living. Only America could do that. Knowing that his cousins in Troy, New York State, would give him a billet, he decided to emigrate. He returned to Ireland in late August to see his family and hold a couple more meetings for the ISRP remnant (now describing itself as the Irish section of the SLP). The wounds were not healed. When he sailed alone for America on 18 September 1903 no socialist came to see him off. Two years later he bitterly recorded his sense of rejection in a letter to Jack Mulray:

If Ireland and the Socialist cause therein ever find another willing to serve them and fight and suffer for them better or more unselfishly than him they cast out, who is now writing to you, they will be fortunate indeed. . . . I regard Ireland, or at least the Socialist part of Ireland which is all I care for, as having thrown me out, and I do not wish to return like a dog to his vomit.

2

In addition to his *Workers' Republic* experience, Connolly had received, some time in 1902 or 1903, formal training as a linotype operator, and he was hoping for work on the *Weekly People* in New York. He was rejected and, for want of a union card, was unemployable anywhere else in that capacity. Nor did the SLP leadership try to help: an immigrant was a very different proposition from a visiting speaker. Finding no welcome in New York, he went to stay with his Troy cousins, found a job as a premium-collector for the Metropolitan Life Insurance Company and joined the local branch of the SLP.

He did not fit in easily. The SLP's main philosophy had been useful to him as a counterbalance to reformism in Britain, but he could not adhere to a party line that did not meet his own Marxist criteria. In March 1904 he wrote a letter to the *Weekly People* critical of party thinking on wages, marriage and religion. He opposed first, on Marxist grounds, its view that wage rises were useless because they would be immediately offset by price rises; secondly, the belief that outmoded monogamous marriage would disappear in a true socialist society; and thirdly, the increasing anti-religiousness of the *Weekly People* — surely socialism had nothing to do with religion. 'I hold', concluded Connolly, 'that mine is the correct SLP doctrine. Now will someone please tread on the tail of my coat?'

De Leon himself took up that challenge. When Connolly's letter was printed in April the editor attacked it personally. He used Marx (wrongly, according to some later Marxist scholars) to prove the short-term nature of wage-rise benefits; declared that the monogamous family owed its origin to property and would be irrelevant in a socialist state; and dismissed Connolly's arguments about the anti-religiousness of the *Weekly People*. There were enough divisions with the SLP to produce plenty of contentious correspondence in the *Weekly People* during the following weeks, including a letter from the Troy branch proposing that Connolly should be disciplined for attacking the party. De Leon proposed a stay of trial until the SLP National Convention in July. Connolly wrote to Matheson that he would 'fight the best I know how', but added that he was perturbed that some correspondents who had written in his support had overstated the dissenting case against De Leon. Meanwhile he sent to *The Socialist* and the Scottish SLP a defence of his own case. Matheson wrote of his envy of Connolly's 'fine, manly, Titanic brutality'.

De Leon won hands down at the convention, which Connolly, being in full-time work and not a delegate, could not attend. He wrote bitterly to Matheson:

> Dan [De Leon] read my correspondence, paragraph by paragraph, *adding his own criticisms in between,* so that the delegates could not discern where I ended and *my quotations* began, and had lost sight of one sentence before he began to read the one that pointed its moral. As a result he had no difficulty in tearing me to pieces.

De Leon's position was endorsed; there seemed no need to discipline Connolly, and the controversy died down for a time. During the winter and the early spring of 1905 Connolly spoke at meetings of a number of New York SLP branches on more or less uncontentious issues.

Connolly was immersing himself in SLP matters even

at a time of great personal trouble. He had had news in June that Lillie was dangerously ill and his children scattered among friends and relations. Although she recovered and his family joined him in August after a year of separation, they brought news of the death of his eldest daughter, Mona, whose dress had caught fire a couple of weeks earlier. Connolly had found a pleasant house in Troy — a far cry from the Dublin tenements — but this blow took the pleasure out of it. A year later he wrote to Matheson:

> I do not like the country, indeed my chief motive in coming here was to provide a better field for my girls than was open for them at home. But the girl for whose immediate benefit the change was made was stricken down by death on the eve of our departure, and the blow darkened my life, and changed all our hopes and prospects.[12]

In later letters America became 'this cursed country'. He was further soured by the loss of his job with Metropolitan Life, leading to yet another separation from his family. (It was rarely that Connolly wrote about his private life. He usually ignored Matheson's friendly queries about his family, and when times were hard, through pride, usually ceased writing altogether.)

He went to New York in late November and spent several months there, finding just enough occasional work to keep the family going, though visits to them were perforce rare. He had, at least, the consolation of friends. He stayed with Jack Mulray, one of those whose opposition had led to the ISRP split. Two impoverished exiles, they met accidentally in New York, buried their differences and became friends. Jack Lyng, who had supported Connolly, was also in town, and they saw a great deal of each other. Connolly had heard from his wife of the great kind-

ness of old ISRP comrades when Mona died. In time
he was able to write to the Dublin associates without [51]
much sign of the old acrimony.

He remained without regular employment until
May 1905, when an insurance company took him on
to find new business on commission in Troy. A major
local strike soon after made that a hopeless proposition – there was no money about in the small community – and Connolly was compelled to move to
where jobs were to be had and his own agitation had
not queered the pitch. In October 1905, claiming to
be an engineer, he started operating a lathe for the
Singer Sewing Machine Company, first in Newark,
where he installed his family, then in Elizabeth, New
Jersey, whither he commuted.

Even the novelty of making an adequate living did
not reconcile him to his continued exile. When
Matheson tentatively asked if he might come back to
Scotland to print and manage *The Socialist* Connolly
explained the trap he was in: he could afford neither
to leave Lillie and the children in America, sending
money to them from a Scottish pittance, nor to ship
them back across the Atlantic. That he regretted this
was clear: 'My wife who was as enthusiastic about
coming here as I was careless is now mad to get out
of the country.'[13] As Matheson pointed out, he was
'growing peevish and crossgrained in that uncongenial
clime',[14] but until some better offer was forthcoming
Connolly was stuck with the United States.

3

In 1905 Connolly was only on the fringes of important new developments in the SLP, but he was taking
a keen interest in the party and its preoccupations.
Despite the challenge to De Leon on wages, marriage
and religion, Connolly still shared his views on the

importance of developing industrial unionism under
party direction. During the 1890s De Leon had despaired of radicalising existing unions and had set up a militantly class-conscious industrial organisation — the Socialist Trade and Labor Alliance (ST&LA) — as a wing of the SLP. By 1905 it had at most 1,500 members, and its main effect was to increase antagonism between the SLP and orthodox unions, particularly the American Federation of Labor (AFL), whose leaders resented being labelled 'fakirs'.

De Leon believed that revolution would come through the ballot box, with industrial unions winning votes by raising class-consciousness, but he was shaken by the falling SLP vote. After a split in the party the SLP was increasingly challenged by the dissenters, who set up the Socialist Party of America in 1901. The SPA aimed at socialist unity rather than Marxist purity and tolerated a broad spectrum of opinion. In 1904 its presidential candidate, Eugene Debs, polled over 400,000 votes as against the SLP man's 31,000.

De Leon realised his influence was waning fast, and at the founding convention of the Industrial Workers of the World in June 1905 incorporated his ST&LA into the IWW. It was consistent with the 'one big union' concept, and through the power of his personality and experience he became far more influential in shaping its policy than the size of his ST&LA membership justified. Fearful lest the IWW become identified with his moderate SPA enemies, he managed to forestall constitutionally any affiliation with any political party. He now accepted the view that industrial unionism was of equal importance with political action in overthrowing capitalism. Indeed, once the revolution had been achieved and the projected 'industrial commonwealth' set up, the 'one big union' would direct the party. De Leon still differed from many IWW members — the anarchist members in particular —

in continuing to believe that political success must precede the overthrow of the capitalist system. [53] Connolly accepted the De Leon view completely. He became a strong supporter of the IWW and in November 1905 wrote that

> All actions of our class at the ballot box are in the nature of mere preliminary skirmishes, and . . . the conquest of political power by the Working Class waits upon the conquest of economic power and must function through the economic organisation.

He agreed with De Leon on the need for political success, but was, if anything, more convinced than his erstwhile mentor that industrial unionism must create within the capitalist system the shell around which a socialist society would eventually be built.

His steady work for the SLP, which continued in speeches and in articles for the *Weekly People* even while he was working fourteen hours a day at the Singer plant, had brought him increasingly into the limelight. He was the chairman of an SLP meeting in New York when De Leon made a speech supporting the IWW, and during the following weeks Connolly, with the help of an Irish immigrant admirer, Patrick Quinlan, held many open-air propaganda meetings on behalf of the IWW. The SPA, meanwhile, had begun to work in Newark in harmony with the SLP, and there were nation-wide hopes that the two parties might ally themselves in a political wing of the IWW. There were, however, irreconcilable differences of principle between the two parties. The SLP believed that henceforward all socialists should join the IWW, while the SPA was prepared to cede to the AFL the workers they had already, while as yet non-organised workers joined the IWW. On this issue the move towards unity foundered.

It was in February 1906 that Connolly's patient

propaganda work gave way to more dramatic activities. Three leaders of the Western Federation of
Miners (backbone of the IWW) — Haywood, Moyer
and Pettibone — suspected of complicity in the
murder of the Governor of Idaho, were kidnapped in
Colorado and taken to an Idaho jail, where they were
held without trial for eighteen months.

There was great anger within the IWW. At a protest
meeting of the New Jersey SLP, at which Connolly
was a delegate, he was appointed to the press and
literature committee. He and Quinlan organised the
Newark Haywood—Moyer defence committee, and
Connolly chaired a Newark protest meeting in April
at which De Leon spoke. Further protest meetings
were organised throughout the rest of the year.

Connolly did not confine his activities to straight-
forward protests and general propaganda. Experienced
in the problems of winning the Irish for socialism, he
sought to apply his skills to another ethnic group ripe
for the SLP and IWW — the Italians. Like the Irish,
the Italians were obsessed with affairs 'at home' and
with the Catholic religion. They did have a socialist
tradition, however, which expressed itself in a journal,
Il Proletario, with endless attacks on the Church and
the clergy. In an attempt to arouse interest in the
Italian socialist community, Connolly taught himself Italian and began translating articles from *Il
Proletario* and publishing them in the *Weekly People*
with prefaces of his own. He spoke often at Italian
Socialist Federation meetings, in Italian when necessary, and appears to have been responsible for drafting
a complaint to the Newark police about their con-
fiscation of red flags. His work had some success.
In July the editor of *Il Proletario* called on readers
to accept that they were American as well as Italian
and to affiliate to the SLP. Connolly, in the columns
of the *Weekly People,* urged that they be encouraged

and got no response. This disappointment compounded his existing resentment at De Leon's dicta-
torial style. 'We are not treated as revolutionaries
capable of handling a revolutionary situation,' he
wrote to Matheson in June, 'but as automatons whose
duty it is to repeat in varying accents the words of
our director general.' He condemned De Leon's failure to make himself dispensable, something which
Connolly always believed to be an important job
of any leader. It was a fair criticism, though Connolly
himself was vulnerable to the same charge.

4

His relatively stable existence as a full-time machine
operator and part-time activist came to an end. By
early 1907 his recruiting work at the Singer plant had
him branded as a troublemaker. Apparently he
resigned rather than jeopardise the job of his fore-
man, who was resisting pressure to fire him.

Whatever the effect this had on his family, Connolly could now concentrate on SLP work. He was
the New Jersey delegate to the SLP National Executive
Committee (NEC) in New York in January 1907. The
NEC meeting saw the beginning of a row between
Connolly and De Leon which had serious reper-
cussions. It began over a trifling matter. De Leon
objected violently to a resolution, proposed by
Connolly, which would give unconditional access
to the columns of the *Weekly People* equally to the
NEC and its sub-committee of members living in or
near New York. When the resolution, ostensibly
drafted for the sub-committee's benefit, was rejected,
it had the side-effect of denying the NEC rights that
had never previously been challenged, and this aroused
the suspicious disapproval of a number of delegates.
De Leon was angry with what he saw as an attack on

his control over the paper he edited. When Connolly [56] and De Leon began to clash they soon developed a strong mutual antipathy, and the respect on which their association had been based evaporated. In letters which he wrote to old ISRP colleagues during the spring of 1907 Connolly denounced De Leon's style of leadership and claimed that it was an American trait to put too much faith in its leaders. He had come, he said, to conclude that 'as revolutionists the Irish comrades are immeasurably superior to anything I have met in America'. He believed now that the best way of winning the Irish in America to socialism was to strengthen the movement in Ireland. He established an organisation in New York for people 'of Irish race and extraction', to educate them in the history of the class struggle in Ireland, keep them abreast of and secure their help for the socialist movement in Ireland and steer them towards revolutionary class-consciousness. This Irish Socialist Federation (ISF) held its first meeting in March and was affiliated to the ISRP's successor, the Socialist Party of Ireland (SPI).

Its inception further exacerbated tensions with the SLP, for De Leon and his followers disapproved in principle, on internationalist grounds, both of ethnic socialist groupings and of Connolly's heterodox view that Marxist teachings must be adapted to varying cultures and traditions if a nation of immigrants was to be effectively mobilised in the cause. There was a long controversy in the *Weekly People,* showing little support for Connolly's position, and his frustrations with the leadership and the party intensified. Simultaneously the row over Connolly's resolution was continuing, with De Leon threatening to resign unless his view of the issue was ratified. The NEC sub-committee was split and Connolly lost the backing of his own State Executive Committee. He was still highly

regarded as a speaker and was selected to address the
May Day 1906 demonstration against 'patriotism, [57]
anti-immigration, Russian Czarism, American Moyer—
Haywood outrages and craft unionism', but he was
smarting too much at his treatment to stay in office.
De Leon, referring to Connolly's 1902 tour, made the
mistake of saying it had been undertaken in the
interest of the British movement. Connolly resented
the implication that the Irish were beggars, more
particularly since the British SLP had not even been
founded at the time in question. He resigned from the
NEC more freely to protest against 'this calumny
upon the Irish movement' and requested the Irish
socialists to publicise the facts of the matter.

These squabbles were of limited interest across the
Atlantic. Several letters to Matheson accused De Leon
of being a bad organiser and anti-proletarian, abusing
the IWW as a recruiting ground for the SLP, and taking
an unjustifiably large salary as editor of the *Weekly
People*. As Matheson remarked, Connolly was clearly
obsessed with De Leon's iniquities, and his new-found
enemies were no less unforgiving. When he sent in
his resignation the NEC was not content to accept
it quietly. After various technical delays the sub-
committee passed a resolution to remove him, condemning him for double-dealing and persecution of
the New Jersey NEC and De Leon.

That should have been the end of the matter; it
was certainly doing the party no good. But De Leon
had not finished yet. Connolly and his family had
now moved to New York, where he was working as
an organiser for the Building and Constructional
Section of the New York IWW. It was hard on the
family (with another new daughter, Fiona) to leave
the pleasant suburbs of Newark for a Bronx tenement,
but there was no alternative other than further in-
tolerable separation. They were still poor: his $18

weekly wage was paid irregularly; but Connolly was [58] enthusiastic about his job and sought to expand his influence far beyond the building trades. He was soon organising tramway-men, moulders, garment workers, milkmen and dockers, and was attracting national attention as the New York correspondent of the *Industrial Union Bulletin.* In addition to his formal duties of making speeches, attending meetings, negotiating and engaging in general propaganda, he spent his spare time with Irish groups, particularly the ISF. In December 1907 he unwittingly set the stage for another confrontation with De Leon.

Connolly was negotiating with the Waterside Workers of New York to bring their 12,000 members into the IWW; the General Executive Board (GEB) of the IWW met in New York on 22 December to discuss affiliation terms. Connolly was absent through illness the following day when De Leon turned up to attack him. Bitter as the feeling was between the two men, Connolly seems to have failed to realise the depth of De Leon's distrust, although it had been made clear at a general meeting of the SLP earlier in the month, when Connolly was accused of incompetence, reformism, personal ambition and divisiveness. Besides, De Leon was genuinely fearful that mass entry of the largely Irish and Italian Waterside Workers would swamp SLP influence in the IWW.

According to a letter Connolly wrote to Matheson in January 1908, De Leon denounced him at the GEB meeting on 23 December as a Jesuit agent seeking to disrupt the IWW by introducing Irish Catholics, having left behind him an Irish career as a wrecker. The GEB, aware of the impropriety of allowing such allegations to be made in the absence of the.accused, notified Connolly to attend the following morning to hear De Leon's charges in person. The GEB found the allegations either irrelevant, unproven or wrong.

Connolly delightedly described De Leon's rout as ending with him finally slinking away 'with his tail [59] between his legs'. It was certainly a setback to De Leon's influence in the IWW.

5

Despite his involvement with the IWW and the SLP, Connolly's heart remained in Ireland, his anger at the circumstances of his departure by now having faded. He made what he feared would be permanent exile endurable by concentrating much of his attention on, and doing most of his socialising with, the Irish-American community — an inadequate substitute for the real thing, as was evident in the frequency with which he wrote to Irish comrades begging for news, seeking to exchange publications and trying to make his activities in America their concern. He hoped that a *rapprochement* might lead them to find him some means of returning.

That concern with his own ethnic group which had got him into trouble with De Leon was symbolised by the work Connolly put into expanding the ISF first through meetings and then through its organ, *The Harp*, which first appeared in late December 1907. Twelve pages long, it was intended to be a monthly, though financial constraints often prevented its appearance. Wryly he chose as a sub-title a Jesuit maxim: 'In things essential, unity; in things doubtful, diversity; in all things charity.' His first editorial regretted the existence in America of two socialist political parties. Had too much emphasis not been placed by both on points of difference, there might now be one great party. Although he could not resist oblique jibes at De Leon, he had no wish to reduce his readership by attacking the party openly (he was, in any case, still nominally a member). He concentrated on issues of concern mainly to Irish-Americans (Protestants, he hoped, as well as Catholics) and preached his new gospel:

> Every one who has the interests of the working class at heart, every one who wishes to see the Socialist Party command the allegiance of the political host of labor, should strive to realize industrial union as the solid foundation upon which alone the political unity of the workers can be built up and directed toward a revolutionary end.

The job of the socialist parties was, he wrote, to continue the assault on the ballot box through propaganda as the industrial movement became stronger and developed its members' revolutionary instincts. The two organisations, when ready, would work together towards the moment when socialism would win control of the state by democratic means. The industrial union, meanwhile, would have built up an industrial republic inside the shell of the political state, ready to set up the true 'workers' republic' — in which the workers would control their own destinies by electing representatives who would, in turn, elect those who controlled the national government.

> Social Democracy must proceed from the bottom upward, whereas capitalist political society is organized from above downward; Social Democracy will be administered by a committee of experts elected from the industries and professions of the land; capitalist society is governed by representatives elected from districts, and is based upon territorial division.

These ideas were developed at length in various issues of *The Harp* and in a lecture on world history designed to prove that the working class was now poised to seize economic control.

Pursuing his avowed policy of adapting theory to established traditions and cultures, Connolly drew on recent Irish history to illustrate the potential of industrial unionism: just as the Land League had harnessed the mass of the Irish people against the landlords, so an entire industry, if the occasion demanded it, could be crippled by a mass strike; whereas, under craft unionism, the lack of class solidarity made the strike an ineffective weapon.

Connolly's determinism did not dilute his determination; his sense of historical inevitability did not bring with it a passive fatalism. He believed in the steady evolution of industrial unionism, but felt it incumbent upon him to speed up the process. In the spring of 1908 he founded IWW propaganda leagues to increase recruitment. De Leon, whose distrust of his opponent had reached new heights, protested immediately to Connolly's employers, the New York Industrial Council, demanding the immediate dissolution of the leagues and the dismissal from his organiser's job of Connolly, a 'police spy'. Connolly retaliated: the slanderer must be expelled from the IWW. Local IWW officials must have been heartily sick of the rows between the two men by this time; certainly they were not prepared to take sides. Both Connolly and De Leon appealed to higher authority and effectively postponed their next bout until the National Convention in September. In the meantime, however, Connolly resigned from the SLP.

It was a hard decision for him to take. Preoccupied with socialist unity, he had rejected the SLP's limitation of its membership to the doctrinally pure, but the existing political alternative, the SPA, was almost a throwback to the SDF — the party he had abandoned in 1903. However, De Leon's intransigence swung the balance, and the SPA's tolerance of his opinions made him feel he could work within it. In

April 1908 he left the SLP and joined the SPA, calling
[62] on Irish voters in forthcoming elections to support
the party which tolerated the greatest freedom of
opinion. He later justified his decision to Matheson:

> At last I made up my mind to join because I felt it
> was better to be one of the revolutionary minority
> inside the party than a mere grumbler out of poli-
> tical life entirely. I would rather have the IWW
> undertake *both* political and economic activity
> now, but as the great majority of the workers in
> the movement are against me in that matter I do
> not propose to make my desires a stumbling block
> in the way of co-operation with my fellow-revolu-
> tionaries.[15]

This acceptance of compromise was significant; the
doctrinally pure socialist of several years' standing
was becoming more pragmatic. (In May 1908, in fact,
he praised Keir Hardie as 'wise in his generation' for
bringing the trade union movement into politics.
Hardie had 'demonstrated to us the real method of
upbuilding a Socialist Labour Party. What we want
to do is to show that the same method can be utilised
in building up a revolutionary party.')[16]
By the summer of 1908 the IWW was in deep financial trouble, an appalling economic slump having
affected disproportionately those at the bottom of
the industrial heap — whence the IWW drew most of
its members. *The Harp* was badly hit, and Connolly
himself could rarely collect his small wage as an IWW
organiser. A contemporary later wrote that in his
struggles to increase the paper's circulation he had
no false pride:

> It was a pathetic sight to see him standing, poorly
> clad, at the door of Cooper Union or some other
> East Side hall, selling his little paper. None of the

prosperous professional Irish, who shouted their admiration for him after his death lent him a helping hand at that time.[17]

As so often before, he resolved to save party, paper and family by a speaking tour. Of all the many cities he visited in several states, only in Boston did he get a good reception. He travelled to the IWW convention in late September on a few dollars borrowed from a New York colleague. Troubled as the IWW was by this time (it could not even afford a stenographer to take minutes), Connolly was impressed by its strong proletarian complexion. Some of the worker delegates had got to Chicago by stealing rides on freight trains. De Leon was anathema to many of the delegates: his intellectual elitism apart, he was not a wage worker and had failed to join his local IWW printers' union. After a four-day wrangle over his credentials, during which he remained defiant, he was excluded. He took his ST&LA and his money away and set up a break-away IWW which achieved little support. Connolly, who had been present to hear De Leon do him the honour of attacking him (among others), received official praise for his propaganda leagues. He was not dismayed by the adoption of this more revolutionary approach to the overthrow of capitalism and the repudiation of political action, since he was convinced that political advance would occur willy-nilly. Connolly was a generous man in many ways, but he had no regrets about the fall of De Leon, despite the great intellectual contribution he had made to the growth of syndicalism in America. His loathing had given way to paranoia: 'Dan has fooled me all along,' he declared, 'and . . . he really is purposely doing the work of the capitalist class.'[18]

[64] Syndicalism was not the only issue to which he addressed himself in the columns of *The Harp* during 1908. In fact, in handling Irish affairs he limited his syndicalist teaching. Too pragmatic now to make the mistake he had made in Dublin — trying to administer the whole Connolly message in one dose — he took a softer, more persuasive line. In writing, for instance, about Griffith's Sinn Féin (We Ourselves) League founded in the previous year to secure political independence through an arousal of national cultural and political self-respect, he criticised only aspects of its policy, while showing a new ability to praise positive virtues in a non-socialist organisation:

> The course of action implied in the name Sinn Féin teaches the Irish people to rely upon themselves, and upon themselves alone, and teaches them also that dependency upon forces outside themselves is emasculating in its tendency, and has been, and will ever be disastrous in its results. . . . Even on the question of the Irish language, Gaelic, a question on which most Socialists are prone to stumble, I am heartily in accord. I do believe in the necessity, and indeed the inevitability, of a universal language, but I do not believe it will be brought about, or even hastened, by smaller races or nations consenting to the extinction of their language.

He even began to learn some Irish himself.[19]

He urged the Irish-American socialist to remain part of his own community, the better to spread the socialist message, which he could do only

> as long as his socialism did not cause him to raise barriers betwixt himself and his fellow countrymen and women, to renounce his connection with, or to abjure all ties of kinship or tradition that through-

out the world makes the heart of one Celt go out
to another, no matter how unknown. [65]

He was taking the middle ground between those international socialists who deplored any manifestations
of nationalism and those Irish people who felt that
the internationalist tenets of socialism made it incompatible with national feelings and traditions. To
members of the latter group he pointed out the
anomaly of the average non-socialist Irishman, who,

> although he would lay down his life for a Church
> which he boasts of as 'Catholic' or universal ...
> turns with a shudder from an economic or political
> movement which has the same characteristics.

He tackled clerical opposition head-on. There was, he
said, absolutely no reason not to be both a Marxist
and a Catholic; when the socialist dawn broke, the
Catholic Church — an immensely adaptable institution
— would be quick to accept and work within the
established order.

This was an issue of such importance to Catholic
communities that Connolly's 'tactfulness in dealing
with such delicate questions as religion' was made a
prime selling point for him in a leaflet issued to SPA
branches by *The Harp*'s publisher, offering Connolly's
services at branch meetings for $5 a lecture. Approving
notices from newspapers were appended, including
the *Boston Herald*'s assessment of his manner as 'that
of an orator and his language that of a scholar'.
Although only a few engagements resulted, Connolly's
growing reputation gained SPA favour. A pamphlet
of his articles on industrial unionism and a selection
of extracts from his 'Home Thrusts' column in the
Workers' Republic and its 'Harp Strings' counterpart
in *The Harp* had been published at the turn of the
year, under the title *Socialism Made Easy* (it was later

to be published in Australia, Scotland and Ireland).
It sold well in socialist circles in America and helped Connolly's reputation and his pocket. The SPA's vague approval turned into concrete action. In April 1908 the national secretary circulated letters to a number of branches asking for lecture engagements for Connolly, whom he described as 'perhaps better fitted' than anyone else to counter Irish Catholic prejudice against socialism. He was by no means acceptable to all opinion within the SPA; the New York section refused to allow the ISF to march in its May Day parade. But the party leadership was more tolerant and appreciative. In June he was appointed as one of the party's six national organisers with a salary (for once regularly paid) of $21 a week. He was assigned to the middle-west and spent about eleven months on tour, lecturing, participating in discussions and advising branches. *The Harp* managed to continue in his physical absence. He continued to supply editorials, and his *Labour in Irish History,* a work on which had had been engaged for a decade, was serialised over many months.

His new job was, he said, the best he had ever had. Nonetheless, Ireland still called him. Quite apart from his family's sense of alienation from America, there was his personal mission. As he put it himself, almost anyone could do his SPA job, but 'there is work to be done in Ireland I can do better than most any one'. Some, at least, of his old comrades agreed with this assessment. Connolly's letters and the publications he had sent them had had a profound effect on their thinking. A youngster in search of enlightenment wrote later of how they had fared:

Round the table sat half a dozen men already known to me by sight. Comrade [Tom] Lyng was there with bowler a-tilt, red tie a-slant, wistful face and flowing moustaches, a mighty haranguer of the multitude.... I asked for pamphlets. Over the mantelpiece, Karl Marx glowers behind his beard, a benign glower.... Under a mellow light emerges the handsome beard and glowing eyes of William O'Brien: he is the only man present who jokes, grimly, with a quiet smile.... One name and one presence pervades the little room: Connolly away in the States. He is the master spirit who has called and held these men together, but somehow they lack his reality and fire.... Only Lyng and William O'Brien seem conscious that they live in Dublin; the rest are a sect conning pamphlets and that long row of Marxist works in the bookcase yonder.[20]

The less adaptable among them must certainly have been sadly confused by their exiled mentor's enthusiastic adoption of yet another new line. The doctrinaire had lost to the unifier hands down. He explained to Matheson how his experience of the SLP had wrought the change:

I have come to the conclusion that, while our position is absolutely sound in theory, and might be sound in practice if adopted by men of large outlook, yet its practical immediate effects have been the generation of a number of sectarians, narrow-minded doctrinaires, who have erected Socialism into a cult with rigid formulas which one must observe or be damned. From whence I draw the further conclusion that our position — the position we started from — needs the corrective of association with Socialists of a less advanced type. In short, I believe that our proper position is in the general Socialist, or rather Labor movement, as friendly critics and *helpers,* rather than in a separate organisation as hostile critics and enemies. It is a bitter lesson to learn, but it is better to learn it than to persist to the end in endeavouring to make statesmanlike Socialists out of a covenanting clique.[21]

In the January 1909 issue of the journal the *Irish Nation* he discussed the Irish socialist reaction to the growth of Sinn Féin. Could they find common ground with Griffith even though he opposed socialism? He urged that an effort be made to do so, and advocated a conference of all socialists (now split between an Irish Socialist Party and a reformed ILP) to evolve a common view and find areas of common interest with Sinn Féin. William O'Brien was inspired to try this, and after a conference in June 1909 the amalgamation of the two groups was announced in August with the foundation of the new Socialist Party of Ireland (SPI). It was committed to independent labour representation on electoral bodies and support for the Irish language, with the ultimate aim of socialism in Ireland achieved through democratic means. Despite the concession on the language, Griffith ignored the overtures. Indeed, he made his antipathy to the new aggression of the labour movement abundantly clear in many public utterances.

Still, the new unity among socialists gave hope for the future, and William O'Brien knew full well who was needed to advance the cause. He wrote to Connolly:

I think it possible to weld all these parties into one body and to double the present membership if there was a man with the necessity tact and ability in the country, and I know of no one who wd more likely succeed than yourself. For this reason I intend to do all I can to enable you to come back here. . . . It seems to me that it wd be possible for you to organise a party of 400 to 500 if you were some time in the country.

There was no doubt about Connolly's enthusiasm for the idea. He was prepared, he told O'Brien, to come [69] back at a tradesman's wage, given some kind of guarantee of basic material comfort for his family. Personal sacrifices for Ireland, yes, but no more slums for Lillie and the children.

He agreed completely with O'Brien that the new party should tailor itself to Irish needs and forget about alliances with parties abroad, and he urged members of the new party to settle their differences internally 'rather than form a number of small parties in which to ventilate said differences'. He seized on a tentative suggestion of O'Brien's that he might bring the publication of *The Harp* home with him. Wasting no time (although O'Brien had been very cautious about the chances of an SPI wage), he immediately sought the approval of the paper's owner, who agreed that Irish and American editions could be printed in Dublin. Connolly asked O'Brien in October to let him know what the printing costs would be.

> You see I am proceeding upon the idea that I am going back to Dublin. Perhaps I am doomed to disappointment. It would break me up completely if I was.

O'Brien was slow to report back, but Connolly went ahead and in December sent to the manager of the *Irish Nation* the copy for the January issue of *The Harp*, telling him that someone from the SPI would provide more copy and arrange distribution. O'Brien was instructed to arrange publicity.

O'Brien was shocked that Connolly should move so far so fast without any word of confirmation from Ireland. Every member of the party he had consulted had disapproved of *The Harp* being transferred without Connolly as editor on the spot.

You appear to assume that there is a demand for the paper here but you are mistaken, as for the present at any rate we think 'The Irish Nation' serves our purpose admirably. Therefore you cannot expect any assistance in running the 'Harp' from the SPI. Under these circumstances the paper cd not be made a success, and I wd strongly urge you to drop the project.

As for the SPI organiser's job, that was out for at least a year.

Connolly's hurt and defiance showed in his response. He inveighed against those who criticised his action. He was transferring the paper to Dublin because printing costs were lower there and would do so even if no copies were sold in Ireland. He would pay a sub-editor. No, he would not make a short trip to Dublin to sort out the SPI problem:

> To take a trip to Ireland to *beg* the comrades there to help me come back permanently — excuse me, friend, I ate that bread once and it was made very bitter. When I go back to Ireland my family will accompany me or I do not go.

Fortunately for Connolly, the editor of the *Irish Nation* saw to the publication of the first Dublin issue of *The Harp,* but there was a long silence from William O'Brien, whose bright ideas had brought him only headaches. In time Connolly's desperate anxiety to get back to Ireland triumphed over his pride. In March 1910 he wrote to O'Brien from Montana that he had been offered an attractive job editing a new socialist/industrial union weekly, which, if he took it, would 'be too engrossing' and he would never get back to Ireland. He was pleased, he said, at the recent news that James Larkin (the labour leader) had assumed management of *The Harp.* He might well make an Atlantic crossing to investigate job prospects.

Over the next few months prospects for such a trip grew brighter. Larkin offered to organise a lecture tour of Ireland for Connolly with some financial guarantees from the SPI, who would also arrange bookings. Connolly took a keen interest, making countless suggestions about towns and organisations in Britain and Ireland he might visit. He was completely committed by early May to arriving in Dublin in late July. His wife had agreed to be left behind yet again, and he was prepared to use his small savings to pay his passage. Although he had finished touring on behalf of the SPA, he did not spend his last months in America in New York in the bosom of his family. In June, at the request of an SPA official, he had gone to Pennsylvania to assist in the defence of the editors of two local papers who had been imprisoned on a technicality after their embarrassingly vocal support for striking tinplate workers. Connolly edited one of the papers, the *New Castle Free Press,* until the editor was released at the end of June.

He stuck to his plan to reach Ireland by late July, despite several pieces of disturbing news from Dublin. Publication of *The Harp* had been suspended pending a libel action againsts its printers (Larkin had incautiously named some names in the June issue). Larkin himself was serving a year's hard labour on various charges arising out of his trade union activities. Boding even worse for the prospects of Connolly's tour, both Larkin and the SPI had been decidedly lackadaisical in their organisation, and there were few bookings. To cap it all, and despite all Connolly had said in letters of the need to make the tour a financial success if he was not to be beggared again, the SPI had lost ground in the previous six months, gone cool on the tour, and drawn the line at the £20 they had already guaranteed. Connolly kept his

temper. 'Cheer up, my boy,' he wrote to O'Brien in
response to his latest doom-laden missive, 'we never
died of a winter yet. Be assured, whatever happens,
no blame is put upon you for not being master of
circumstances. I'm not kicking.'

On 14 July the ISF held a farewell dinner, and two
days later Connolly sailed for Ireland. The trip
inspired him to write some verse in the maudlin style
he affected. His interest in literature was limited, and
his songs and poems (a selection of songs was published in America in 1907) were rooted firmly in the
long Irish tradition of rousing patriotic ballads of no
literary merit. Yet it is unfair to sneer at the unpre-
tentious; Connolly simply enjoyed a rousing and
nostalgic song, and the trite words of this one — 'The
Call of Erin' — cannot disfigure the sincere devotion
which was carrying him away from prosperity back to
penury. A typical stanza read:

> With the engines 'neath us throbbing,
>   And the wind upon our stern,
> Little reck we of the distance
>   That divides us now from Erin.
> For we hear her voices calling —
>   Sweeping past us to the West —
> Calling home to her the Children
>   She once nourished on her breast.[22]

4
Hope

1

Two important works of Connolly's (both written in
America), *Labour, Nationality and Religion* and
Labour in Irish History, were published in Ireland
shortly after his return in July 1910. He was an
established pamphleteer, well aware of the ephemeral
nature of his newspapers and unwilling to see all his
carefully argued prose disappear into oblivion. A
review of the pamphlets shows the trends in his
political thinking. Apart from his first venture – the
edition of selections from Lalor – he had by 1910
already published three pamphlets both in Ireland
and America. The first (1897) edition of *Erin's Hope*
was an attempt to reconcile social democratic socialism
with republicanism; the 1902 edition combined De
Leonism and republicanism. Republished in 1909, it
drew criticism: Connolly, an IWW member, had dealt
only with the political organisation of the workers
and not the economic. Connolly replied ruefully:
'Our reviewer forgets that the book was first printed
in 1897. We confess to have learnt something since.'
The New Evangel Preached to Irish Toilers, a selection from his articles in the *Workers' Republic,* was
published as a pamphlet in 1903 (though the articles
come from 1899 only) and dealt with his main preoccupations of that period: the dangers of middle-
class reform, the distinction between state monopoly
and socialism, the importance of a political party
representing the class interests of the masses, and, a

foretaste of controversies to come, the separation
between socialism and religion. *Socialism Made Easy*
(later reprinted with changes as *The Axe to the Root*),
which contained articles published between 1898 and
1909 — many of them revised — was largely designed
to popularise his syndicalist views.

Labour, Nationality and Religion was written during
Connolly's last months in America in response to a
series of Lenten discourses against socialism given in
Dublin in 1910 by a Jesuit, Father Robert Kane. The
Catholic bishops of Ireland were deeply disturbed by
the strikes and upheavals caused by Jim Larkin's new
union and were concerned to nip in the bud what
they saw as an attempt to wean the Irish masses away
from spiritual to materialistic values. The Dublin
socialists felt threatened by the massive publicity
given to Father Kane's swingeing and detailed indict-
ment and looked to Connolly for a counterblast.
Connolly was used to clerical attacks and had frequently answered them in articles and speeches, but
to his extensive rebuttal of Father Kane he applied
the best of his mind and a great deal of research. He
was uniquely qualified, not only by his intellectual
qualities but also because he was known to be a
Catholic who had always rebuked the anti-religious
socialists. It is ironic that Connolly, the champion of
the Catholic's right to be a socialist, was not himself
a believer. In 1908 he had written to Matheson:

> For myself, tho I have usually posed as a Catholic
> I have not gone to my duty for 15 years, and have
> not the slightest tincture of faith left. I only
> assumed the Catholic pose in order to quiz the
> raw freethinkers whose ridiculous dogmatism did
> and does annoy me as much as the dogmatism of
> the Orthodox. In fact, I respect the good Catholic
> more than the average freethinker.[23]

He must have long been aware that it was vital, if he wished to extend his influence in Irish and Irish emigrant circles, to maintain the pose. He was realist enough to give due weight to the high value the Irish placed on their religion, and recognised that they would accept only a brand of socialism complementary to it. Not that he was cynical. He had a sincere appreciation of the important role the Catholic religion had played in developing Irish race-consciousness, and he found his own lack of belief no handicap in defending Catholicism against socialists and socialists against clerics. De Leon's endless accusations against Connolly's supposed religion had no doubt stiffened his resolve to maintain the 'pose', much as certain non-believers declared themselves Jews when the Gestapo called at their doors.

The pamphlet was masterly: a combination of careful research and devastating logic. He chose to meet Father Kane on his own ground by using Catholic history and the early Christian fathers against him. In tackling recent attempts by clerics to have socialists excommunicated, he began by reminding Father Kane and his fellows of their place. An important point of Catholic doctrine was

the almost forgotten, and sedulously suppressed one, that the Catholic Church is theoretically a community in which the clergy are but the officers serving the laity in a common worship and service of God, and that should the clergy at any time profess or teach doctrines not in conformity with the true teachings of Catholicity it is not only the right, but it is the absolute duty of the laity to refuse such doctrines and to disobey such teachings. ... It is this saving clause in Catholic doctrine which has again and again operated to protect the Church from the result of the mistaken attempts of the clergy to control the secular activities of the laity.

In a telling thrust:

> It seems to be unavoidable, but it is entirely regret-
> table, that clergymen consecrated to the worship
> of God, and supposed to be patterned after a
> Redeemer who was the embodiment of service and
> humility, should in their relation to the laity insist
> upon service and humility being rendered to them
> instead of by them. Their Master served all Man-
> kind in patience and suffering; they insist upon all
> Mankind serving them, and in all questions of the
> social and political relations of men they require
> the common laity to bow the neck in a meekness,
> humility and submission which the clergy scorn-
> fully reject.

He went on to list almost twenty examples of stances
by the papacy or the Irish hierarchy recognised by
many respected Catholic laymen, contemporaneously
or later, to be wrong, including clerical attacks on the
American War of Independence, on the 1798 rebellion and on peaceful attempts to have the Act of
Union repealed, and papal defence of English con-
quest and rule of Ireland. The Catholic Church, he
argued, had adopted capitalist values completely
divorced from the principles upon which it was
founded. He quoted, among others, St Gregory the
Great ('The earth of which they are born is common to all, and therefore the fruit that the earth
brings forth belongs without distinction to all'), St
Chrysostom ('The rich man is a thief') and St Ambrose
('It is only unjust usurpation that has created the
right of private property'). He dealt in detail with
Father Kane's misrepresentations of socialist thinking
and aims and stressed the spiritual values which per-

meated its thinking — to co-operate 'knowing no
rivalry but the rivalry of endeavour toward an end
beneficial to all' — as he also stressed the material
aspect of Christ's mission. Scrupulous as he was in
arguing his religious points wholly by reference to
precedents in Catholic teaching, he made no concessions to clerical sensibilities. Some of Father
Kane's arguments were described variously as claptrap
and blasphemy. His assault on Pope Leo XIII's en-
cyclical against socialism, *Rerum novarum*, began:

> If one of the boys at the National Schools could
> not reason more logically than that he would
> remain in the dunce's seat all his schooldays.

The whole pamphlet was Connolly at his best —
authoritative, lucid, penetrating, humorous and
unafraid. Although criticised by secularist socialists
as being inconsistent with Marxist theory — owing
more to Catholic than to socialist teachings — it was
a pragmatic and powerful corrective to the prevailing
Catholic fear of socialism.

In *Labour in Irish History* Connolly once explained his reasons for expending so much effort
on the hibernicisation of Marxism:

> Each country requires a local or native literature
> and spoken propaganda translating and explaining
> its past history and present political developments
> in the light of the knowledge derived from a study
> of Socialist classics.
>
> Any country which is content to depend solely
> upon these great Socialist classics will never have a
> Socialist movement of the working class; it may
> have a Socialist sect of a few true believers, but it
> cannot hope for the adhesion of the great mass of
> the toilers.

In *Labour in Irish History*, his most ambitious

work, he sought to make a fundamental contribution.
[78] It was an immensely demanding piece of work — the application of Marxist thinking to the history of Ireland — the history of the vast mass of the Irish people. It set out

> to do what in us lies to repair the deliberate neglect of the social question by our historians, and to prepare the way in order that other and abler pens than our own may demonstrate to the reading public the manner in which economic conditions have controlled and dominated our Irish history.

The two propositions on which it was founded he declared to be:

> [First,] that in the evolution of civilisation the progress of the fight for national liberty of any subject nation must, perforce, keep pace with the progress of the struggle for liberty of the most subject class in that nation, and that the shifting of economic and political forces which accompanies the development of the system of capitalist society leads inevitably to the increasing conservatism of the non-working-class element, and to the revolutionary vigour and power of the working class.
>
> Second, that the result of the long drawn out struggle of Ireland has been, so far, that the old chieftainry has disappeared, or through its degenerate descendants has made terms with iniquity, and become part and parcel of the supporters of the established order. . . . Only the Irish working class remain as the incorruptible inheritors of the fight for freedom in Ireland.

He believed that the book 'could justly be looked upon as part of the literature of the Gaelic revival'.

It was by any standards a remarkable achievement. Leaders dominated the current Irish conception of their history as monarchs dominated in the English mind. Possessed of hardly any formal education, Connolly was challenging the historians at their own game, yet his survey of Irish history in detail from the late seventeenth century to his own time showed evidence of wide reading and mature reflection. It was not all a record of oppression and misery. In one of the most interesting chapters he drew an optimistic lesson for the future from the success of a co-operative association at Ralahine, Co. Clare, set up by a disciple of Robert Owen, an Irish landlord called Arthur Vandeleur. In the few years of its existence, before Vandeleur lost his estate through gambling, it was prosperous, harmonious and non-sectarian. Connolly believed that

> In the rejuvenated Ireland of the future the achievement of those simple peasants will be dwelt upon with admiration as a great and important landmark in the march of the human race towards its complete social emancipation.

It proved that socialism could work in practice in the most unpromising conditions.

It was not, of course, history in its academic, modern sense. It bore the twin imprints of economic determinism and Connolly's own bitter hatred of the middle-class nationalist tradition. What did not fit in with his theory — nineteenth-century Ulster and its anti-nationalistic Protestant masses, for instance — was ignored. His villains were deep-dyed, his heroes unsullied, his idealisation of early Gaelic civilisation romantic. But that was typical of the historical writing of the time; what was new and important was the book's application of international thinking to the Irish situation. Connolly's reading and travels had given him vision far beyond insular Irish society. He took an interest in — and wrote about — exploitation

and socialist developments throughout the world.
[80] Where most of his contemporaries developed ideas
out of their Irish experience, his ideas came from
outside and gave him an articulate and novel perspec-
tive on the country's past and future. The Ireland
that greeted him on his return from America did not
yet recognise his stature, but the socialists, at least,
were aware of a phenomenon outside their experience.

His old comrades found him changed. He was more
confident, mature and compassionate, and less dog-
matic, though still tending to irascibility. In appearance too there were the alterations of middle age.
Seán O'Casey has left us a memorable picture of the
man, and incidentally of a propaganda meeting typical
of hundreds he held throughout his life as an agitator.
O'Casey was a critic of Connolly's, but his account
is in its way a moving tribute. A lifetime of effort
in a cause that more often attracted apathy than
enthusiasm had won some converts who were prepared to follow him to their deaths.

A tiny group of men followed Jim Connolly through
the streets . . . a large slouch hat covering Connolly's
head, a large round head, fronted by a rather
commonplace face, its heaviness lightened by fine,
soft, luminous eyes; the heavy jaws were jewelled
with a thick-lipped, sensuous mouth, mobile, and
a little sarcastic, bannered peacefully by a thick
and neatly-trimmed moustache. His ears were well
set to the head, the nose was a little too thick, and
gave an obstinate cast to the bright eyes, and a firm
fleshy neck bulged out over a perfectly white hard
collar. The head and neck rested solidly on a broad
sturdy trunk of a body, and all were carried forward on two short pillar-like legs, slightly bowed,
causing him to waddle a little in his walk, as if his
legs were, in the way of a joke, trying faintly and

fearfully to throw him off his balance. Silent, he walked on, looking grim and a little surly, followed by the tiny dribble of followers, one of them carrying a box so that, when Connolly spoke, he might be lifted up before the people as he preached the gospel of discontent smoking faintly in the hearts of most men. Up on the box, the soft slouch hat came off, and the hard, sparsely-covered head turned this way and that, the mobile mouth flickered with words, red with the woe of the common people, words that circled noisily over the heads of the forty or fifty people hunched clumsily together to oppose the chill of the wind.

2

Labour in Irish History had concluded on a syndicalist note, condemning the 'merely political heresy under which middle class *doctrinaires* have for nearly 250 years cloaked the Irish fight for freedom'. Drawing on the precedents of earlier struggles, Connolly's conclusion was that

> Irish toilers from henceforward will base their fight for freedom not upon the winning or losing the right to talk in an Irish parliament, but upon their progress towards the mastery of those factories, workshops and farms upon which a people's bread and liberties depend.

There was now the problem of harmonising his syndicalist ideas with the SPI, which was committed to simple political advance.

James Larkin had changed the face of Irish trade unionism by the time Connolly returned. Liverpool-born of Irish emigrant parentage, he had been a highly successful organiser in Britain for the National Union of Dock Labourers, which in 1907 dispatched him to Ireland, at the age of thirty-one, to reorganise dock labour there. Like Connolly, he was a socialist and a nationalist; like the public Connolly, a Catholic; like the recently emerged Connolly, a syndicalist, though more in practice than theory. In Belfast he had shaken traditional union conservatives to their foundations, crossing — alas briefly — sectarian dividing lines and raising the self-confidence of the workers to a level which resulted in widespread strikes, rioting and disruption. From 1908 he was based in Dublin, where he soon had a membership of nearly three thousand. At the end of the year, suspended by his own executive, who could not take his individualistic and headlong approach to union organisation, he founded his own union, the Irish Transport and General Workers' Union (ITGWU), with himself as general secretary, taking many members of his old union with him. The idea was to create a militant working-class movement which cut across craft and other divisions. In *The Harp* Connolly was propounding a philosophy of syndicalism which Larkin had moved towards almost by instinct.

Larkin was not Connolly's intellectual equal, but in his own way he was a man of equal stature; in O'Casey's words, 'He was far and away above the orthodox Labour leader, for he combined within himself the imagination of the artist, with the fire and determination of a leader of a down-trodden class.' He had a passion for social justice, and like Connolly before him, despite a British slum background, he was appalled by the degradation of the life of the Dublin poor. Larkin was more a demagogue than Connolly, and though they had so many experiences and aspirations in common, their personalities were too different and too well defined for them to work easily together. Yet they appeared natural allies when

Connolly returned to Ireland — Connolly in sympathy with Larkin's actions, Larkin with Connolly's thinking. [83] Virtually Connolly's first meeting after arrival in Ireland on 26 July was with Larkin in Mountjoy Prison, at Larkin's request. He undertook to help with the campaign for his release. After a reception in his honour in Dublin and two weeks of reunions and speeches he set off on a tour which took him to Belfast, Cork, Liverpool and a number of Scottish towns.

His mature prose style was matched by his mastery on the platform. A contemporary wrote:

> He was not exactly a great orator, although he could rise to oratory too. But he had a method, a style, a manner that exactly fitted and adorned the splendid material he used in his speeches. He was never slipshod, never flamboyant, but always earnest, simple and informative. . . . From Connolly you got a cogent, coherent and reasoned statement of a case, presented in the clearest manner, illustrated by the most telling allusions, with the argument marshalled in the coldest and calmest fashion, yet warmed with the burning fire of sincerity and sympathy. . . . The effect of Connolly's oratory was remarkable. If it did not arouse the wild and whirling enthusiasm evoked by the outburst of a demagogue, it created enthusiasm of a different kind. It compelled assent as well as respect, it carried conviction and it aroused enthusiasm of the more lasting kind, a quiet, enduring enthusiasm which forced the hearer to act on Connolly's side rather than cheer his words.[24]

Or as another put it, 'Larkin knew how to draw a crowd but Connolly knew how to hold one.'[25] His worth to the SPI was quickly proved; by the end of

August 1910 he had established branches in Belfast [84] and Cork.

The SPI offered him a job for six months at a wage of about £1 15s a week, regretfully rejected as insufficient for his family's needs, though he stressed his enthusiasm for the party. To O'Brien's suggestion that Larkin might give him a job (he was about to be released) he reacted with dignity: 'I was glad that I was able to initiate the move that led to his release but don't want to demand a price for it.' O'Brien worked on in Dublin trying to find a way of saving Connolly for the movement, but in the end it was Larkin who solved the problem. After his release he met Connolly in Glasgow to discuss the matter, convinced that the money could be found somewhere in the labour movement. Connolly, unwilling to go on the ITGWU payroll for fear of undermining his position in the SPI, and disheartened by the shilly-shallying of the party executive, decided to return to America. At the eleventh hour the SPI, goaded into action by Larkin, issued an appeal for funds and guaranteed Connolly £100 a year — enough, when supplemented by his earnings as a lecturer and writer, to have him writing to Lillie on 13 November:

> This is the fatal letter. I want you to come back to Ireland. . . . I am sure that I have a more promising future in Ireland than in America, not so often and so long away from home as I would be if we stayed in the US. You are not coming back to the misery you left. Do not be afraid of that.[26]

Lillie's trust in him, after all the vicissitudes, allowed her no choice. His appreciation of all the sacrifices she had made for him was never in doubt; her patience and resilience over many years earned at least token recognition in the inscription in the copy of *Labour in Irish History* he sent her early in November: 'To my dear wife, the partner of all my struggles and the inspirer of my achievements.' Lillie and the family [85] packed up and were in Dublin by early December, where, as promised, they were decently housed. A large welcoming party was organised by the colleagues and friends of earlier days.

The SPI manifesto was issued about this time. Although it made reference to the need for the Irish working class to 'organise itself industrially and politically with the end in view of gaining control and mastery of the entire resources of the country', it was primarily concerned that socialists gain political ground by supporting 'every honest attempt on the part of organised Labour to obtain representation through independent working-class candidates pledged to a progressive policy of social reform'. Connolly must have been involved in its drafting; he was content to push for the lowest common socialist denominator. Jim Larkin was getting on with making a reality of syndicalism, and there were myriad nationalist forces at work, so Connolly's job was still to make socialism acceptable to the mass of the Irish people, subordinating theory to compassion.

One of his early initiatives on returning to Dublin as SPI organiser was to approach two women's groups, the Women's Franchise League and Maud Gonne's Inghinidhe na hÉireann, to seek their help in pressing for the extension to Ireland of new legislative provisions for feeding poor schoolchildren. The help was gladly given, and as an interim measure both groups set up soup kitchens of their own. Connolly was greatly admired among feminists. No one could doubt his deep commitment to the women's suffrage movement, for which he campaigned throughout his life. He had shown himself happy to accept women as comrades in action, valued them on their own merits — whether they be the gentleness and devotion of his wife, the energy and flamboyance of Maud Gonne, the oratorical skills of his ISF colleague, the young Elizabeth Gurley Flynn, or the organisational powers of his eldest daughter, Nora. He addressed himself in his prose to 'working men and women' and sent messages of fervent support to suffragette meetings. 'When trimmers and compromisers disavow you,' he wrote in one, 'I, a poor slum-bred politician, raise my hat in thanksgiving that I have lived to see this resurgence of women.' It was no wonder that some of his staunchest admirers came from feminist ranks, especially in a country where they got short shrift.

3

Early in 1911 Connolly set about activating public opinion in the far south on the school meals issue (a deputation to the Home Secretary was being organised), but he had reckoned without the Catholic conservatism of that part of the country. Cork was hostile; Queenstown (now Cóbh) was enraged. When he tried to speak there in early March he was denied the use of the City Hall, and at the open-air meeting organised instead he came under heavy attack. One stalwart asked him if he had written that the Jesuits killed popes. Connolly's stout-hearted reply did nothing to win converts in a clerical stronghold:

> This is an appeal to prejudice, but I will not be intimidated. My answer is that Father Kane the Jesuit denounced us in his Lenten lectures and I wrote a reply showing that the mud he had thrown at us could be more fitly thrown at him and his Order. The Jesuits and Dominicans were expelled from many countries for political intrigue.

A shout of 'What about free love?' went up, and the mob charged, smashing Connolly's soap-box. Saved

by the arrival of the police, Connolly headed back to
Cork. Despite police advice, he returned a few days [87]
later, but was accorded not even a brief hearing.
Amid the clatter of tins and buckets, shouts of
'Atheists!' could just be heard. When the crowd eventually charged, Connolly and his colleagues escaped
in a sidecar through a hail of missiles, with the mob
at their heels. He described Cóbh, with feeling, as
'that nest of parasites feeding upon parasites'.

In succeeding weeks Connolly had more on his
mind than the failure of his southern mission: the SPI
financial guarantee had proved hollow. On a visit to
Edinburgh he told John Leslie that he was thinking
of settling in England. Leslie assured him that if he
returned to Ireland he would yet 'find a niche in the
hall of fame'. Dublin was impossible at current unemployment levels; the alternative was Belfast. His
daughter Nora accompanied him there.

He quickly joined the tiny Belfast branch of the
ITGWU, but failed to get elected as a delegate to the
ITUC, where he had planned to support the setting up
of an Irish labour party, free of any British connection. The majority at the conference, to his disgust,
backed the established party, part of the British ILP,
and one of its leaders, William Walker. Writing in the
Scottish socialist journal, *Forward* (to which he contributed regularly for more than four years from late
1910), he condemned the Belfast ILP's conception
of internationalism as 'scarcely distinguishable from
imperialism', in its

attempts to treat as one, two peoples of whom one
has for 700 years nurtured an unending martyrdom
rather than admit the unity or surrender its national
identity.

He was soon involved in controversy with Walker,
a powerful labour leader who had been a prime

influence in resurrecting the near-moribund Belfast
Labour Party — coming close to winning a seat a few
years previously. There was no common ground
between Walker, a Unionist and an enthusiast for
municipal socialism, and Connolly, who in Walker's
view was a bad internationalist. The debate turned
vicious. Connolly attacked him on Marxist grounds,
but Walker (and, after his departure in 1912, the
Walkerites) budged not an inch. The opposition
Connolly met in trying to seduce the people of
Belfast with schemes for a socialist republic can
hardly have come as a surprise.

He was still jobless, and by the time he had moved
his family to lodgings near the Falls Road at the end
of May he was also heavily in debt to friends.[27] With
some of his old bitterness he wrote to the treasurer
of the SPI:

> Mrs Connolly is under the impression that when
> the Dublin comrades got us out of Dublin they left
> us to starve, as she has already been 3 days in
> Belfast, a strange town, without a penny to buy
> food.[28]

It is unclear how he intended to make a living. Nora
Connolly, who was working in a linen mill, has
recorded how furious he became at a suggestion that
he could live off his children. Certainly his only
serious prospect seemed to be a job with the prosper-
ing ITGWU, which was now in a position to afford a
full-time organiser in Belfast.

Connolly's faith in Larkin had received some blows
in the past: Larkin's brief editorship of *The Harp* had
turned it into a hard-hitting labour publication instead
of the more intellectual socialist propaganda sheet it
had been under Connolly, and the subsequent libel
actions in 1910 had contributed to the paper's demise.
In May 1911 Connolly wrote to O'Brien (who had

Larkin's ear) to complain that Larkin had never invited him to take part in any demonstrations while he was in Dublin: 'The man is utterly unreliable – and dangerous because unreliable.' The knife was twisted in the wound when, In June 1911, Larkin launched the hugely successful *Irish Worker,* which quickly secured a steady circulation of over 20,000 a week. Its popularity was unsurprising. Where Connolly had dealt in ideas, Larkin voiced specific grievances and delighted his readers by singling out bad employers by name.

While waiting for a job to come up Connolly spoke in Dublin as part of the campaign of protest against the forthcoming visit to Ireland of the new King, George V, and drafted a manifesto which echoed his fulminations against the visit of Victoria a decade earlier, couching it in language so strong that its distributor was jailed for three months. Amid its political arguments it called on fellow-workers to 'stand by the dignity of your class. All these parading royalties, all this insolent aristocracy, all these grovelling, dirt-eating capitalist traitors, all these are but the signs of disease in any social state.'

Back in Belfast, he was not idle for long. In early July Larkin had urgent need of an organiser there, and O'Brien had been championing Connolly. Larkin sent him a telegram with two weeks' pay appointing him to the job.

4

From the early summer of 1911 the British Isles were rocked by a wave of unparalleled industrial militancy. After years of high unemployment, first under Conservative governments and then under a Liberal majority backed by Labour, many sought an alternative to political action. With an improvement in trade in 1911 the time was right to strike for better pay and conditions. The British labour movement had firmly resisted industrial unionism, but despite its intrinsically divisive craft basis, many of its unions were sufficiently strong, and discontent sufficiently widespread, to start a major assault on the employers using the near-syndicalist weapon of sympathetic strikes. Transport workers were followed out by railwaymen, seamen and firemen by dockers, coal-fillers and carters. By the end of June every British port — and Belfast as well — was closed. Strike fever spread quickly to Ireland.

Connolly was soon involved. On 19 July he brought out three hundred Belfast dockers in sympathy with the cross-channel seamen and promptly put forward claims on their behalf. He led parades through Belfast to the music of recruits from Catholic and Orange bands, collecting money for the strike fund. With help from Dublin he was able to make small strike payments for a couple of weeks. The Belfast Trades Council pledged support, and as attention was focused on the appalling wages and conditions of Belfast dockers (15s a week for backbreaking work was typical), public sympathy swung towards them. In the face of the solidarity of the dockers and their allies in other unions, the employers offered a com-promise settlement, including recognition of the union and an average weekly increase in pay of 3s a week. Connolly, aware that union money would not last through a long strike, accepted with delight. Larkin had had similar successes in Dublin. And the driving impetus — the general spirit of industrial unrest — was still spreading from Britain; events were overtaking the leaders of the ITGWU and other unions. They could not have withstood the pressure for strike action even if they had wanted to. During the following six months workers in a wide range of industries in towns all over Ireland staged so many strikes that the employers began to unite against them in a national organisation. Larkin's union was still comparatively small (about 8,000 in 1912), but its rate of growth, its transcendence of normal craft lines and Larkin's socialism, personal popularity and fighting rhetoric led employers to see him and his union as their main enemies.

Connolly's amenability to members from all sources extended in early October to female mill workers — some of them relatives of his docker members — who had come out in protest against restrictive rules which forbade them, among other things, to sing, talk, laugh or bring sweets into the mill. Most mill workers were unorganised, and the existing linen workers' union, led by Mary Galway and catering mainly for the better-off Protestant workers, denounced the strike. Connolly demanded the abolition of the rules and a pay rise and held a series of meetings to encourage solidarity. One of them he described with pride:

The girls fought heroically. We held a meeting in St Mary's Hall and packed it with 3,000 girls and women. They were packed from floor to ceiling, squatting on the floor between the platform and the seats — 3,000 cheering, singing, enthusiastic females, and not a hat among them. The following resolution was passed unanimously: 'Resolved: That this mass meeting of mill-workers welcome the establishment in this city of a textile branch of the IT and General Workers' Union, and that we pledge it our unfailing and undivided support; and that we condemn as a disgrace to our civilisation the conditions sought to be imposed upon us by the mill-owners and heartily endorse the strike in the mills and recommend the strikers to the sympathy and support of the Belfast public.'

With the help of the brass band, a little money was
[92] raised for strike pay at 2s a week. Connolly was
attacked not just by the official union but by local
clergy. Nora, who persuaded him to go to mass one
Sunday during the campaign, sat in shock while the
priest gave a sermon against Connolly and his labour
activities. Connolly, inured to such attacks, sat
through it unmoved.

The mill workers had to go back with their demands
unmet, but Connolly's ingenuity rose to the occasion.
He advised concerted action to flout the regulations:
if one transgressed, all her workmates should follow.
The strategy was so successful that the rules became
a dead letter. At the end of November, despite
the opposition of Miss Galway, he set up a textile
workers' section of the ITGWU.

Despite these occasional successes, it was uphill
work developing the union in Belfast, where sectarianism tended to limit membership to Catholic
workers. Peak membership during Connolly's in-
cumbency — at the time of the dock strike in June
1911 — was between 600 and 800. While workers
would join for a week or a month in time of need,
poverty made them prone to drop out when the crisis
was over. Connolly could hope to maintain the size of
his roll only by continuous effort and the acceptance
of a shifting membership.

Circumstantial limitations notwithstanding, he had
proved himself too useful to be left undisturbed in
Belfast. The ITGWU had been involved since August
1911 in a lockout of foundry-men in Wexford by
employers who refused to let them join Larkin's
union. With ITGWU dock workers on strike and the
importation of blackleg labour, local tensions were
high. Organised by P. T. Daly, an SPI member on
Larkin's staff, the foundry workers stood firm,
backed up financially by sympathisers in many parts

of Ireland. Parades ended in violent battles with the police; one worker was beaten to death. Daly was arrested and moved to Waterford at the end of January 1912, and Larkin sent Connolly to Wexford to try to settle the five-month-old dispute. He brought peace within two weeks by intelligent compromise: an Irish Foundry Workers' Union was formed, later affiliating with the ITGWU. The employers, conscious of the depth of local feeling against them, accepted this defeat as a face-saving victory. Connolly remained in Wexford until his campaign to have Daly released succeeded, meanwhile laying the foundations of the new union and holding recruiting meetings throughout the county.

Back in Belfast in March, he had time to spare from trade union activities, for 1912 was a quiet year in industry. With trade booming and the disruptions of the previous year fresh in their minds, employers in Britain and Ireland were conciliatory and workers disinclined for further confrontations. In his ITGWU role Connolly concentrated on maintaining the loyalty of his textile and dock workers. He held open-air meetings at which funds were raised for the textile workers' section (12s 6d a week was the autumn peak). Dancing classes were introduced in June to add a social dimension to union activities. Although the membership of both his unions was largely Catholic, Connolly fought against the ever more deeply entrenched sectarianism of Belfast: in July he organised a labour demonstration under ITGWU auspices, proclaiming it as 'the only union that allows no bigotry in its ranks' and leading to the meeting place a procession of dockers and mill workers headed by what was now called 'The Non-Sectarian Labour Band'. Regular Sunday-evening meetings were held thereafter. He tried to increase membership in the textile trade in November by issuing an appeal,

entitled *Linen Slaves in Belfast,* urging the workers
to organise to secure the minimum hourly rate of
3d, but with little success in expanding membership.
His major contribution in that year was to socialist
politics, not industrial unionism.

5

The Liberal government was committed to bringing in
a Home Rule Bill in the spring of 1912. With the delay-
ing powers of the House of Lords — the old enemy of
Home Rule — reduced to two years, nationalists all
believed that some measure of Home Rule would be
in force by 1914. Although he still disliked the Irish
Parliamentary Party, Connolly had come to believe
that any measure of independence was better than
none and saw clearly the need to create a labour
party to represent working-class interests in an Irish
parliament. He had already laid the groundwork by
speaking as an SPI member at ILP branches on the
need for unity.

He organised a conference in Dublin at Easter 1912
to discuss the foundation of a united party. It was
attended by delegates from SPI branches in Dublin,
Cork and Belfast, from four ILP branches in Belfast
(Walker's branch did not respond to the invitation)
and from the Belfast branch of the British Socialist
Party (an ILP/Social-Democratic hybrid). It got off to
an unfortunate start when the BSP delegation walked
out in protest: a Dubliner had substituted the Union
Jack for the doormat. The conference gave birth to
an Independent Labour Party of Ireland (ILP(I)) and
accepted the programme which Connolly had drafted
for it — avoiding controversial issues. Republicanism
was not mentioned, and syndicalists and social demo-
crats were equally catered for. The party was to work
towards an 'industrial commonwealth' based on

common ownership of land and instruments of pro- [95]
duction, distribution and exchange, and with complete social and political equality for women. This
was to be achieved on two fronts: by winning office
in all public elective bodies (including the expected
Irish parliament) and by furthering unity of action
in the industrial field. The party, formed as 'the
political weapon of the Irish working class' was to be
open to all men and women 'irrespective of their past
political affiliations'.

The tolerant tone of the programme was typical of
the new Connolly. In a letter to a worried comrade he
rebuked him for 'cultivating the mind and methods
of a little religious sect quarrelling about points of
doctrine' and for paying too much attention to
American socialist controversies:

> American programmes, phrases and parties are no
> more applicable to Ireland than the programmes,
> phrases and parties of Ireland are applicable to
> Timbuctoo. Hence, why get excited about them?
> When I was in America I took a very decided stand
> on one side, but if I was to meet in Ireland to-day a
> man who took the opposite side I would fraternise
> with him and forget about our feuds.

He spelled out once and for all his conception of
syndicalism:

> Syndicalism is simply the discovery that the
> workers are strongest at the point of production,
> that they have no force available but economic
> force, and that by linking the revolutionary move-
> ment with the daily fight of the workshop, mill,
> shipyard and factory the necessary economic force
> can be organised. Also that the revolutionary
> organisation necessary for that purpose provides
> the frame-work of the Socialist Republic. Upon

that point all Syndicalists are agreed and nothing
else is necessary to make a Syndicalist. . . . As long
as we agree upon the essential point why cavil
about others? And the essential point is a belief in
the wisdom of organising the economic power of
the workers for the revolutionary act.[29]

The Home Rule Bill was published on 11 April
1912 and pleased no one. To the Ulster Unionists,
their faces set against the breaking of the Union, it
was of its very nature a betrayal; to Redmond it was
deficient in not giving an Irish parliament control
over finance; to more radical nationalists it was an
insulting half-measure at best. Connolly attacked it
roundly at a meeting of the Belfast branch of the
ILP(I), demanding that it be reworked to provide for
proportional representation, payment of members
and women's suffrage, and that the proposal to establish an upper house be dropped. He also accused the
Redmondites of conniving at the gerrymandering of
constituencies. His proposals were all accepted —
except for women's suffrage, for which he was often
a lonely fighter.

He could reasonably feel satisfied with the ILP(I),
but he saw it primarily as a socialist propaganda
organisation which must be augmented by a party
linked closely to the unions. In May, at a meeting of
the ITUC, he proposed a resolution:

That the independent representation of Labour
upon all public boards be, and is hereby, included
amongst the objects of this Congress; that one day
at least be hereafter set apart at our annual gathering for the discussion of all questions pertaining
thereto; that the affiliated bodies be asked to levy
their members 1s per annum for the necessary
expenses, and that the Parliamentary Committee

be instructed to take all possible action to give effect politically to this resolution.

It was cleverly conceived and worded. No mention was made of socialism, which would have alienated some members. As it was there was considerable opposition from some of the craft unions. But with Home Rule, as they thought, upon them, and a concomitant urgency in the preparation of a Labour opposition, the majority in favour of the resolution was almost three to one.

The establishment of this machinery, from which the Irish Labour Party later sprang, was one of the most practical of Connolly's achievements. His delight in it was alloyed by the long period of inaction that followed. Larkin, who had enthusiastically supported the resolution and who, as chairman of the parliamentary committee, was responsible for translating it into action, lost interest. He had been elected in January 1912 to the Dublin Corporation along with four other Labour candidates, but after several months was debarred as a convicted felon. If he could not because of the law be personally active in politics, he could summon up little enthusiasm for it. He continued to support candidates representing the labour movement, but devoted most of his energies from then on to his union.

Connolly was upset to learn from the faithful William O'Brien that despite all efforts, no progress had been made in establishing an Irish labour party. At the initial meeting of the parliamentary committee Larkin had resigned over disagreement with one of his rulings. He refused to chair a meeting called by O'Brien in September to push things along. Connolly wrote that the general inactivity since the Congress had made him 'sick and sorry I ever returned'. He could not speak at the meeting himself because he feared that Larkin would accuse him of neglecting his Belfast duties.

> I begin to fear that our friend Jim has arrived at his highest elevation, and that he will pull us all down with him in his fall.

> He does not seem to want a democratic Labour movement; he seems to want a Larkinite movement only. . . . He must rule, or will not work, and in the present stage of the Labour movement, he has us at his mercy. And he knows it, and is using his power unscrupulously, I regret to say. We can but bow our head, and try to avert the storm. . . . I am sick of all this playing to one man, but I am prepared to advise it for the sake of the movement.

Larkin did speak at the September meeting — rather destructively. With the impetus lost, the ILP(I) received no further attention from the unions for many months.

During 1912 Connolly had time to develop his ideas on the need for the Irish labour movement, in its new, broad sense, to reclaim Ireland for its ordinary workers of all creeds. These ideas were expressed in open-air speeches over many months from the spring of 1912, published in the *Irish Worker* and printed in 1915 as a pamphlet, *The Reconquest of Ireland.* The common people of Ireland, he argued — Catholic and Protestant — had been robbed of their land and their civil rights; social injustice was responsible for an appalling degree of poverty and deprivation (the death rate of the Dublin poor was higher than Calcutta). *The Reconquest of Ireland* was mainly a programme of action for the proposed Irish labour party. The chief end of such a programme was an improvement in the people's lot, and all those sympathetic to that end must collaborate. It stressed the sufferings of Protestant workers at the hands of capitalists, and of Nonconformists under religious persecution, for Connolly was responding to the sectarianism which surrounded him and the mounting opposition in parts of Ulster to Home Rule, which was shaking his and many other nationalists' confidence in the inevitability of that long-awaited independence. Sir Edward Carson, a compelling orator, had become the leader of Unionist forces in Ireland and at Westminster, dedicated to killing the Home Rule Bill. Backed by the Conservative opposition, the Unionists were making it clear that they would not confine themselves to parliamentary opposition. In September 1912 Carson led a great mass of Ulstermen in signing the Solemn League and Covenant, both an expression of loyalty to the King and a pledge to use all necessary means 'to defeat the present conspiracy to set up a Home Rule Parliament in Ireland'.

Connolly was impervious to the virtual hysteria generated. A colleague of his in Belfast later described how, during one of Connolly's open-air lectures, he was interrupted by a militant Unionist:

> Drawing a copy of the Solemn League and Covenant from his pocket [he] brandished it in the air and remarked there would be no Home Rule for Ireland and that he and his thousands of co-signatories would see to it. Connolly, with a sardonic smile, advised him to take the document home and frame it, adding 'your children will laugh at it'.[30]

But the groundswell of opinion was against him, and he had nothing to offer the Protestants but an invitation to join in the labour movement of the Irish nation, admitting that the vast mass of Protestants, duped as they were by capitalism and imperialism, were unlikely recruits. Home Rule would come, though, with or without their goodwill.

Even after so long in Belfast, Connolly had not
[100] preceived the depth of fear and suspicion in Ulster
Protestants. There, as in Scotland and America, he
had spent most of his time in Irish Catholic communities, and those few Protestants he knew well
in Belfast were almost all socialists. Yet his airy
dismissal of Unionism was more than ignorance: it
was an example of his penchant for believing what he
needed to believe. He had elaborated an incontro-
vertible intrepretation of the inevitable progress of
Irish history. How could it be upset by an anomalous
dissident movement virtually confined to the north-
eastern corner of the country?

6

Towards the end of 1912 Connolly took time to
reply to another Jesuit assault, this time from Father
MacErlean in the *Catholic Times,* who accused him
of ignorance and misrepresentation in *Labour,
Nationality and Religion* and attacked his central
thesis on the compatibility of Catholicism and
socialism. Others joined in, and the correspondence
deteriorated into a wrangle over the role of the
Church in specific historical events. The socialists
won on points.

At the end of the year, with Belfast Trades Council
backing, he decided to run for the city council.
Standing in a ward in which the ITGWU was strong,
he adopted a simple reformist programme, but also
declared his socialism, his belief in Irish independence
and his support for women's suffrage. Backed by
most socialists, Catholics, nationalists and trade
unionists (including some who were anti-Home Rule),
he won 905 votes to his Unionist opponent's 1,523,
after enduring violent censure from both anti-socialist
Catholics and anti-Catholic Protestants.

Larkin was going from strength to strength as 1913 brought a fresh sense of industrial disaffection. He became union master of the ports and by mid-1913 had an overall membership of about 14,000, based mainly in Dublin. Relations with Connolly were poor.

> I don't think I can stand Larkin as a boss much longer. . . . He is for ever snarling at me and drawing comparisons between what he accomplished in Belfast in 1907, and what I have done, conveniently ignoring the fact that he was then the Secretary of an *English* organisation, and that as soon as he started an Irish one his union fell to pieces, and he had to leave the members to their fate. He is consumed with jealousy and hatred of anyone who will not cringe to him and beslaver all over him.[31]

Another source of irritation was Larkin's administrative carelessness. The ITGWU had registered as an 'approved society' under the National Insurance Act. Connolly's insurance staff were paid from Dublin, and their salaries were often in arrears. He had a number of disputes with Larkin over financial matters and on one occasion hinted at resignation. O'Brien wrote to him, in Larkin's defence, of the tremendous personal strain caused by remorseless press invective against him.

At the ITUC meeting in May 1913 Connolly was one of those behind the forming of a permanent committee, whose brief included drafting a constitution for the proposed party. His interventions at the Congress included an attack on the gerrymandering in the Home Rule Bill, condemnations of the coercion of suffragettes and a demand for the extension to Ireland of the medical benefits contained in the Insurance Acts.

In Belfast too 1913 was proving a memorable year

on the union front. In June Connolly wrote to O'Brien:

> I am in the midst of strife and tribulation here, a strike on in the brickworks, 300 men out, a strike in Larne, the same number out, and a rival union established on the docks to fight us — the Belfast Transport Workers' Union. This is an Orange move, fostered by the employer. . . . I see ahead the fight of our life.

The Larne strike collapsed in the face of exhortations from Protestant clergy to go back to work. Connolly knew what he was up against:

> Our transport members here are not near so good a class as they have in Dublin, and the feeling of the city is so violently Orange and anti-Irish at present that our task has been a hard one all along. . . . Our fight is a fight not only against the bosses, but against the political and religious bigotry which destroys all feeling of loyalty to a trade-union.[32]

The ITGWU and textile union's joint outing in August bore him out. On their return the trippers required police protection to escape a crowd of Orangemen (estimated at 10,000) who hurled sticks and stones at them as they left the station.

On 29 August he received a telegram summoning him to Dublin to assist in the all-out industrial war between employers and workers.

5
Disappointment

1

In August 1913 Larkin's power was at its height. He controlled almost all unskilled labour in Dublin, many agricultural labourers throughout the county and significant groups in other parts of Ireland. His own and his union's popularity were enhanced by a string of successes over wages and conditions. With most employers taking a relatively soft line, prospects seemed bright for ITGWU members, but Larkin was riding high. He felt ready to take on his chief enemy, William Martin Murphy, Ireland's richest employer.

There was a deep personal antagonism between the two men. Murphy's *Irish Independent* denounced Larkin as an atheist; Larkin's *Irish Worker* lambasted Murphy as a 'blood-sucking vampire'. It was not surprising that Murphy (who by Dublin standards was a good employer) reacted savagely when Larkin tried to organise the workers in his Dublin United Tramway Company. He refused to recognise the union, and in mid-August began to dismiss suspected Larkinites from the Tramway Company and the *Irish Independent*. By the use of pickets Larkin persuaded many retailers to black the *Independent,* and when the largest newspaper distributors in Ireland, Easons, continued to sell it he called a strike within the firm. His dockers then refused to handle any consignments from Easons. On 26 August nearly half the tram workers walked out at Larkin's instruction. At a public meeting that evening Larkin said: 'By the living God, if they want war they can have it.' Two days later he, [104] William O'Brien, P. T. Daly and two other members of the ITGWU were arrested for seditious libel and conspiracy.

Connolly arrived in Dublin on Friday 29 August in time to participate in an evening public meeting, where Larkin (out on bail) burned a proclamation banning a demonstration to be held in Sackville Street on the following Sunday with the words 'People make Kings and people can unmake them.' Fearing arrest, he went into hiding, and Connolly reminded the crowd that there was nothing to stop them strolling through Sackville Street on Sunday to see if a meeting was taking place — ban or no ban. On Saturday he and a colleague were arrested, as was Larkin at the Sunday meeting, which was followed by riots in which 400 people were injured: the police, their patience strained by the battles with strikers the previous day, struck out brutally even against wholly uninvolved members of the public. The savagery of the scenes in Sackville Street and the news that two men had died in the weekend fighting drew public attention in Britain and Europe to events in Dublin. Murphy raised the temperature further. He rallied the members of the Employers' Federation to lock out employees who refused to sign a pledge not to join the ITGWU. By 22 September 25,000 men were out of work; taking their families into account, about 100,000 Dubliners faced starvation.

The employers had perhaps been encouraged by the news that Larkin was remanded in jail and Connolly had been sentenced to three months. The Dublin authorities, though, were fearful of stirring up more trouble: Larkin was again out on bail by 12 September, and Connolly was released two days later after a week on hunger-strike, undertaken though frustration at being out of things. (He was the first

Irish political hunger-striker.) After a few days spent recuperating he took over while Larkin was away in Britain canvassing support from the British labour movement. On a visit to Dublin (during which he visited Connolly in jail) Keir Hardie offered help, and a British TUC committee of investigation reported that the right to join a trade union was at stake. From late September the BTUC and other sympathisers began to raise money — some £150,000 in all — for the Dublin workers. Food ships began to arrive in late September, and food and clothes centres were set up under the direction of Larkin's sister, Delia, founder of the Irish Women Workers' Union, and Countess Markievicz.

Constance Markievicz, born into an Anglo-Irish Ascendancy family, had the energy, beliefs and compassion to make her active in many causes. Women's suffrage, Sinn Féin, Inghinidhe na hÉireann and her boyscout organisation (the Fianna Éireann) had all attracted her work and devotion. More important was her loving work for the poor. She admired Larkin, but it was Connolly who became her inspiration. They had both been involved in the protest against the visit of George V in 1911, and their friendship had begun in the following year when she stayed with the Connollys in Belfast. It was to her home that he was driven when released from jail in September, and it was there that he normally stayed when visiting or living in Dublin from this time onwards (his family did not leave Belfast until his death) — his pride dictatating that he give her 10s a week for his keep.

Two days after the arrival from Belfast of the first food ship a Board of Trade court of inquiry was opened under the chairmanship of Sir George Askwith, one of their most able arbitrators. Connolly helped prepare the statement of the workers' case, but the star of the hearing was Larkin, whose impassioned presentation of that case took almost two hours to deliver.

[106] The employers, he said, were defending a system which allowed over 100,000 people to huddle together in putrid slums, but 'we are determined that Christ shall not be crucified in Dublin'. The report of the court was published on 6 October. It proposed that in exchange for the withdrawal of the Murphy pledge and the reinstatement of the locked-out men there should be an agreement not to have sympathetic strikes for two years. The employers rejected the recommendations. They would not negotiate until the ITGWU was 'reorganised on proper lines' with new officials. It was clear they would do no deal with Jim Larkin.

The writer George Russell ('AE') spoke for many when in an 'Open Letter to the Dublin Employers' he anathematised their insolence, ignorance and inhumanity. They might win, he said, but that would ensure their own damnation.

> The men whose manhood you have broken will loathe you, and will always be brooding and scheming to strike a fresh blow. The children will be taught to curse you. The infant being moulded in the womb will have breathed into its starved body the vitality of hate. It is not they — it is you who are blind Samsons pulling down the pillars of the social order.

2

With public opinion behind him more strongly than ever Larkin went to Britain to try to win workers there to sympathetic action. Speeches he had made there in September had been intemperate, but there was no moderation at all now. He launched a vicious attack on the Labour Party for its opposition to sympathetic strikes, declaring them to be 'about as useful as mummies in a museum', and encouraged [107] union members to defy their leaders and strike. He also gave his blessing to a well-intentioned plan by suffragettes to bring children of strikers to Britain to be looked after. Connolly, who had been to Scotland briefly on a similar errand, arrived back in Dublin on 28 October to find that Larkin had been jailed for seven months. Archbishop William Walsh had condemned as unworthy of the name any mother sending her children 'to be cared for in a strange land without security of any kind that those to whom the poor children are to be handed over are Catholics'. Priests were picketing boats to England, and two of the suffragettes had been arrested for kidnapping. Larkin had named Connolly as his substitute, and all problems were landed in his lap.

Larkin had been prepared to defy the clergy. Connolly, more the realist, knew when to admit defeat, but, having called off the plan to ship the children out, he suspended free meals at Liberty Hall (ITGWU headquarters) and told his supporters: 'Go to the archbishop and the priests. Ask them for food and clothing.' When the archbishop, the clergy and Catholic charitable organisations responded with help Connolly resumed the free meals.

Dublin employers seemed likely to negotiate if Connolly replaced Larkin; British union leaders also favoured Larkin's deposition. But loyalty (and, of course, the fervent pro-Larkinism of the workers) dictated that Connolly should instead organise a campaign for his release from jail. In meetings in Dublin he preached solidarity and resistance to British labour's anxiety for peace at any price. At a gigantic meeting in the Albert Hall in London, where speakers included George Bernard Shaw, George Lansbury and George Russell, Connolly proposed that every sympathetic

person vote and work against the Liberal Party —
[108] despite its sponsorship of the Home Rule Bill — in the three forthcoming by-elections: 'It doesn't matter whether it is a Labour man or a Tory that is against the Liberal. The immediate thing is to hit the government that keeps Larkin in jail.' His argument appealed to a wide spectrum of public opinion. Larkin had been jailed for seditious libel at a time when Sir Edward Carson was promising a treasonable revolt if the Home Rule Bill became law. Even some Liberal newspapers were pressing the government to release him. Following government defeats in the three by-elections, Lloyd George said: 'There are explanations, the most prominent of which is, probably, Jim Larkin.' On 13 November he was released.

Connolly had displayed less tactical sense in dealing with a crisis at the docks, through which some employers had begun to import blackleg labour from Britain. Connolly had earlier threatened that in such an event 'Dublin will run red with the blood of the working classes.' Now that it was happening, he called for mass picketing and, when that failed, closed the port of Dublin, thus violating — however understandably — an agreement with the Steampacket Company, giving strength to the employers' claims of ITGWU irresponsibility and uniting them more than ever. Connolly was undeterred. Larkin had announced at Liberty Hall on his release from jail that the employers of Dublin would 'sup sorrow with a long spoon'. Connolly followed up:

> We will carry on the fight until we have demonstrated that the Transport is going to rule the roost here in Dublin and throughout Ireland.

That cry did little to calm the fears of those who saw the ITGWU as dangerous syndicalists.

Larkin and Connolly needed more than financial and moral support from their British allies. They issued a joint manifesto appealing to members of British trade unions to find ways to keep the port of Dublin closed, and Larkin repeated the call in a speech in Manchester. On 18 November Larkin and Connolly asked the parliamentary committee of the BTUC to block the importation of non-union labour into Ireland and to hold up Dublin-bound goods. The labour leaders were suspicious that Larkin was working up to a demand for an all-out sympathetic strike. The decision was referred to a special session of the BTUC on 9 December. Larkin heightened their alarm over the next few weeks, insulting some of them by name and appealing directly to their rank and file. (Some of them had stopped spontaneous sympathetic action by their members.) Connolly was nearly as damning. He referred publicly to 'labour leaders who were . . . only old fossils, and were willing to sell the pass any time'. Two days before the TUC meeting a peace conference in Dublin collapsed over the question of the reinstatement of all locked-out workers.

The TUC special meeting opened gently enough with a bid by the British for some say in peace negotiations. Connolly replied peaceably and made a good case for the ITGWU's refusal to give way on the reinstatement issue. Although he refused to withdraw criticisms made of the British leadership, he avoided raising any personal issues, but that was not enough to defuse a resolution condemning the 'unfair attacks made by men inside the trade union movement upon British trade union officials'. Bitter recriminations against Larkin followed, and he replied with equal venom to the 'foul, lying statements'. He was certain, he said, that the British rank and file would support their fellows in Dublin. The upshot was a resolution to reopen negotiations without concessions on the question of sympathetic action in Britain. Connolly [110] answered for the Dublin delegation with dignity:

> I and my colleagues from Dublin are here under a deep sense of humiliation. It would have been better for the conference to have first endeavoured to try and settle the Dublin dispute and afterwards wash their dirty linen. The reverse has however been the case.

Larkin announced that they would fight on, but the Congress decision was a crippling blow to the Dublin resistance. Attempts to renegotiate with the employers got nowhere. The Dublin dockers were ordered back to work, as shipping had started to use Derry as a back door into Ireland. Funds from Britain dwindled to almost nothing. There was a general sense in the British labour movement that it had all gone on too long, that Larkin was uncontrollable and that forces were being unleashed that they could neither contain nor approve.

There were reports of a quarrel between Larkin and Connolly. In order to scotch such rumours and create an impression of unity, they made a public appearance together in early January 1914 and issued a joint manifesto calling for more financial support and declaring that the struggle would continue. It was an empty declaration. The workers, starving and desperate, were drifting back to work. When, in February, the BTUC announced that no more funds would be forthcoming, it was the end. Connolly wrote in *Forward:*

> And so we Irish workers must again go down into Hell, bow our backs to the lash of the slave driver, let our hearts be seared by the iron of his hatred, and instead of the sacramental wafer of brotherhood and common sacrifice, eat the dust of defeat and betrayal. Dublin is isolated.

Humiliating though it had been for Connolly to watch the collapse of the workers, he found some comfort in the long battle. In November 1913, when he was still hopeful of success, he wrote of the triumphant story that should be told of the strike — how the women wage-slaves had joined with the oppressed labourers 'to express the will to be free',

how the spectacle of the slave of the underworld, looking his masters in the face without terror, and fearlessly proclaiming the kinship and union of all with each and each with all . . . caught the imagination of all unselfish souls, so that the skilled artisan took his place also in the place of conflict and danger, and the men and women of genius, the artistic and the *literati*, hastened to honour and serve those humble workers whom all had hitherto despised and scorned.

The response of the men of letters had indeed been overwhelming. George Russell had become a friend. Connolly wrote of his 'great genius and magnetic personality' and enthused about his ideas for extending the activities of the agricultural co-operative societies to forge links with industrial workers. Shaw, Yeats and other Irish writers had shown deep sympathy with the workers' fight. For many of them, the revelations in the press about the conditions in which the poor lived in Dublin were new and shocking. The writer and schoolmaster Patrick Pearse, who up to 1913 had had little interest in social matters, had his eyes opened:

Twenty thousand Dublin families live in one-room tenements. It is common to find two or three families occupying the same room; and sometimes one of the families will have a lodger! There are tenement rooms in Dublin in which over a dozen persons live, eat and sleep. The tenement houses of Dublin are so rotten that they periodically collapse upon their inhabitants, and if the inhabitants collect in the street to discuss matters the police baton them to death. . . .

Can you wonder that the protest is crude and bloody?[33]

In welcoming the support of middle-class *literati* like Pearse, as he had welcomed that of the aristocratic Maud Gonne and Constance Markievicz, Connolly was going against the grain of his own class hatred, often expressed in articles, poems and songs exhorting others not to forgive or forget. He was admitting now, in deeds if not in public words, that he was learning to accept help where it was sincerely offered.

Even in February, when it was all over, he was not in absolute despair. The Murphy pledge, on which the whole battle had been fought, often proved unenforceable, and, more important, the exhibition of class solidarity in Dublin and in Britain gave great hope for the future. He still believed that the British workers had been squarely behind their Dublin comrades, however pusillanimous their leaders.

The propagandist toils on for decades in seeming failure and ignominy, when suddenly some great event takes place in accord with the principles he has been advocating, and immediately he finds that the seed he has been sowing is springing up in plants that are covering the earth. To the idea of working-class unity, to the seed of industrial solidarity, Dublin was the great event that enabled it to seize the minds of the masses, the germinating force that gave power to the seed to fructify and cover these islands.

I say in all solemnity and seriousness that in its attitude towards Dublin the Working-Class Move- ment of Great Britain reached its highest point of moral grandeur — attained for a moment to a realisation of that sublime unity towards which the best in us must continually aspire.

In an article in April, 'Old Wine in New Bottles', Connolly continued his excoriation of the working class's leaders. The wave of sympathetic strikes in 1911, he declared, had been a success in practice for the ideas of industrial unionism, and trade union amalgamations had given great hope for future labour solidarity, but the trade union leaders were retreating into a new form of sectionalism and a cowardly campaign against spontaneous strikes — which were essential to the success of the labour movement.

It was a syndicalist's article, but Connolly still held the view that political action remained crucial:

A new social order cannot supplant the old until it has its own organisation ready to take its place. . . . Therefore I am heart and soul an Industrial Unionist. But because I know that the Capitalist class is alert and unscrupulous in its use of power, I do not propose to leave it the uncontested use of the powers of the State.

And finally, in a revealing sentence:

Because I realise that human nature is a wonderful thing, that the soul of man gives expression to strange and complex phenomena, and that no man knows what powers or possibilities for good or evil lie in humanity, I try to preserve my receptivity towards all new ideas, my tolerance towards all manifestations of social activity.

A significant new manifestation was the new labour

defence force. Concerned by the violence of the struggles between police and workers, Captain Jack White, a workers' sympathiser, had proposed on 12 November 1913 the introduction of a drilling scheme for those locked out. The idea struck a ready chord in Connolly. During a speech delivered on the following day at a meeting celebrating Larkin's release from jail he announced:

> Listen to me, I am going to talk sedition, the next time we are out for a march, I want to be accompanied by four battalions of trained men with their corporals and sergeants.[34]

On 23 November two companies were created, and Captain White began to drill the Irish Citizen Army (ICA) regularly. Five hundred men were enrolled within a short time.

The ICA was only one example of the pervasive militarism evident in late 1913. A year earlier the Unionist resistance to Home Rule had thrown up a military organisation which became the Ulster Volunteer Force. One hundred thousand strong and increasingly effective, it pressed home to nationalists the seriousness of the threat to Home Rule and added substance to the spectre of partition, now being publicly debated as an alternative. The need for a counterforce became evident. Accordingly, a fortnight after the Citizen Army was proposed, the Irish Volunteers were established. They had a wider appeal than the ICA and grew swiftly to a membership of many thousands. ICA membership dwindled with the end of the lockout, but the ITGWU leadership was determined to keep the little force in being. In March 1914 a written constitution was adopted, the organisation was tightened up, and Larkin held a number of recruiting meetings over the next few months. The ICA had its own flag — the Plough and the Stars.

Connolly was in Belfast once more, caught up in politics and more alert now to the seriousness of the sectarian divisions within Ulster. Violence and victimisation had increased in Belfast during 1913, and he was distressed to see that Catholic as well as Protestant bigotry was growing. In July he had still believed that reason might prevail:

> The Irish question is a part of the social question, the desire of the Irish people to control their own destinies is a part of the desire of the workers to forge political weapons for their own enfranchisement as a class.
>
> The Orange fanatic and the Capitalist-minded Home Ruler are alike in denying this truth; ere long, both of them will be but memories, while the army of those who believe in that truth will be marching and battling on its conquering way.

In September, admitting that the Orangemen had had no written guidance acceptable to them, he wrote an article incorporating a socialist interpretation of an event from Ulster history illustrative of the exploitation of Protestant by Protestant.

In March 1914 he was forced by events to take more seriously the Unionist opposition to Home Rule: not only were the Ulster Volunteers now armed, but in that month a group of army officers at the Curragh, Co. Kildare, announced that they would resign rather than fight them. The Liberal government, dreading open rebellion in Ulster, were to compromise by amending the Home Rule Bill to exclude, temporarily, part of the province of Ulster, Redmond accepting reluctantly that this was the only way to get Home Rule on to the statute book. Connolly saw this as a betrayal, cynically stage-managed by Liberals, Irish Parliamentary Party and Unionists. If the Crown were to withdraw completely, he wrote, 'the Unionists could or would put no force into the field that the [116] Home Rulers of all sections combined could not protect themselves against with a moderate amount of ease'.

Faced with a choice of loyalties — class or religion — most Ulster workers chose the latter, as Connolly now realised. His dislike of Belfast and his disillusion with most of its people were evident:

> Belfast may or may not go to war, but if she does she still wears the outward appearances of respectable mediocrity and slave-driven wagedom. There is none of the enthusiasm of rebellion for a holy cause. . . . Here are only the signs and symbols of a people who have pawned their souls for a usurer's promise of prosperity.

In the *Irish Worker* he sounded a more militant note when he wrote that against partition 'Labour in Ulster should fight even to the death if necessary, as our fathers fought before us.' With the labour movement split in Ulster and badly weakened in Dublin by the lockout, the rhetoric of revolt stopped at rhetoric.

His hopes of opposition to partition from the British labour movement proved equally illusory. The parliamentary Labour Party accepted the line of the Irish Parliamentary Party. Connolly refused an invitation to speak at a May Day meeting in Glasgow and wrote in *Forward:*

> I cannot this May Day felicitate you or the working class of the world in general on the spread of working-class solidarity. Instead of it I see much mouthing of phrases, much sordid betrayal of our holiest hopes.

He had been bitter enough against the British labour leaders when they failed to give total support to the

ITGWU in its time of trial. Now his bitterness was compounded and expressed in verse:

> Aye, bitter hate, or cold neglect
> Or lukewarm love at best
> Is all we have or can expect
> We aliens of the west.

4

The tensions between Larkin and Connolly were still in evidence, although their attitudes to the new crisis were equally militant. Connolly's short temper betrayed itself at a meeting in June, where he and Larkin were to speak simultaneously from different platforms. Larkin began to speak before the appointed time, and Connolly refused in pique to utter a word. Both men made amends: Larkin by praising Connolly lavishly in his mistimed speech, and Connolly by writing in *Forward* that 'Jim was never in better form.' It reflects well on Connolly that he stood by Larkin as loyally as he did. Relations between the two were never good; there was frequent divisive pressure from many directions; and Connolly never ceased to distrust the Irish passion for leaders. He knew too, without false modesty, that his judgment was frequently better than Larkin's. Yet he did not intrigue against him even when complaining to intimates, nor did he ever seek to supplant Larkin himself. He recognised always that, for all his demagoguery, Larkin was a vital force within the labour movement, whose personal style, compassion and rhetoric did more for labour solidarity than any number of good organisers or wise men.

Larkin took the chair at the meeting of the ITUC on 1 June 1914 which launched the Irish TUC and Labour Party. Connolly attacked the failure of the

British Labour Party to oppose partition, and a resolution condemning it was passed overwhelmingly. He
made a number of other contributions and was elected
to the national executive committee. It was some
small consolation to him at a time of great disillusion
that after a two-year delay the Irish Labour Party had
at last come into being.

Larkin's behaviour continued to cause concern. He
was suffering badly from strain and overwork and was
threatening to leave Ireland permanently. He was
capricious, eccentric and difficult in personal relation-
ships. Connolly made it clear to William O'Brien that
he was genuinely anxious that Larkin should stay in
Ireland: his presence was vital for the cause. At a public meeting held in late June in Dublin to persuade
Larkin, who had resigned from his post, that the union
was loyal to him, Connolly spoke of him with feeling
as 'the best man our class has turned out in Ireland'.
'Jim knows I am no follower of Larkin. . . . I am with
him as a comrade, and I believe he accepts me as such.'
Trivial objections had been made to Larkin's actions,
he said, but he would not support Jim's opponents.
For his health's sake, and hence the movement's, he
should do less work. The meeting ended with the
burning of Larkin's resignation.

Although Larkin's health improved during the
summer, his dissatisfaction with Ireland continued.
He decided to go to America on a speaking tour. It
was generally felt within the union that a break might
restore his balance, though some of the officials, Connolly included, were worried about sending him to
the US as a representative of the ITGWU in his unpre-
dictable state. Larkin was determined to go anyway,
and by September the trip was no longer in doubt.
Connolly was the obvious choice to succeed and Larkin had seemed to recognise it, but in late September
he changed his mind and informed Connolly on a visit

to Belfast that he would recommend instead P. T. Daly (his loyal lieutenant for many years). Connolly, he [119] proposed, should be placed in charge of the *Irish Worker* and the Insurance Section. Connolly found this wholly unacceptable. He believed Daly evaded difficulties and would end the emergent friendship between anti-Redmond nationalists and the union. He thought he could not himself serve under Daly — even if that meant losing his job. 'That the control of the Insurance Section should be left to *me* is incomprehensible, except on the supposition that it was given me in order to concentrate upon me the *unpopularity* which that nasty job entails.'[35] On 9 October he wrote to Larkin explaining his position:

> During the very critical period of last year's fight you placed me in charge, and to bring me to Dublin now and put me in a position subordinate to Daly would be equal to announcing to the public that you had come to the conclusion that I was not fit to be trustee. I do not think I deserve this, and it would help to convince a good many that you had been influenced by the attempts of your enemies to sow dissension amongst us, and had fallen headlong into their trap.

He would prefer to stay away from Dublin than serve there under Daly, where he would 'share the responsibility of the failures without the power to avert them'.

Larkin gave in under pressure from the Executive Committee. When he left Ireland for America on 24 October 1914, ostensibly on a fund-raising trip, Connolly took over as general secretary, editor of the *Irish Worker* and commander of the ICA. Larkin was expected back the following year. He did not return until 1923.

5

On 4 August 1914 Britain declared war on Germany. It was to Connolly the ultimate capitalist betrayal of the masses:

> This war appears to me as the most fearful crime of the centuries. In it the working class are to be sacrificed that a small clique of rulers and armament makers may sate their lust for power and their greed for wealth. Nations are to be obliterated, progress stopped, and international hatreds erected into deities to be worshipped.

He was aggrieved, though he cannot have been wholly surprised, when the resolutions of the Second International to oppose war by workers' action proved to be hollow. All over Europe socialist groups joined their own national war efforts.

> What then becomes of all our resolutions: all our protests of fraternisation; all our threats of general strikes; all our carefully-built machinery of internationalism; all our hopes for the future? Were they all as sound and fury, signifying nothing?

Only Lenin's Bolsheviks, the Serbs and the Irish remained true to the resolutions. That the Irish did so owed much to the instransigent anti-war stance of Larkin and Connolly. 'Stop at home,' said Larkin. 'Arm for Ireland. Fight for Ireland and no other land.' Connolly was equally militant:

> I know of no foreign enemy in this country except the British Government. Should a German army land in Ireland tomorrow, we should be perfectly justified in joining it, if by so doing we could rid this country for once and for all from its connection with the Brigand Empire that drags us unwillingly to war.

In September, maddened by Redmond's support for Britain's war effort, he echoed the old tag that 'Eng- land's difficulty was Ireland's opportunity':

> If you are itching for a rifle, itching to fight, have a country of your own; better to fight for our own country than for the robber empire. If ever you shoulder a rifle, let it be for Ireland. Conscription or no conscription, they will never get me or mine. . . . Make up your mind to strike before your opponents.

This clear commitment to physical force was a departure for Connolly. Although from the outbreak of the Boer War he had never absolutely ruled it out, he had wanted no part of it. The retreat of the European socialists, the failure of trade unions to act against a capitalist war, and the success of the Ulster Volunteers in securing partition by threats, all combined to make him despair of achieving without violence the future he had worked for so long. He was in no way mollified when Home Rule received the royal assent on 18 September. The provisos — that it should be suspended for the duration of the war, and after that until a special amendment had been passed to deal with Ulster — precluded any feelings more positive than a grim satisfaction that the imperialist—capitalist conspiracy was running true to form.

In his last few weeks in Belfast, before leaving to take over from Larkin, he made efforts to rouse anti-war feeling, but the Belfast labour movement was fast following its British comrades into support for the war. Some of Connolly's few supporters were nervous about his extreme statement.

> They seem to have a curious idea of what constitutes working-class propaganda. They don't seem to think that I ought to express an opinion on the

greatest crisis that has faced the working class in our generation.

His open-air propaganda meetings on behalf of the Belfast ILP(I) were stopped by members afraid of Orange violence. It was fortunate that Connolly was about to leave Belfast, for, as he wrote to O'Brien, 'I am sick, Bill, of this part of the Globe.'

Isolated from his old British socialist helpmeets, Connolly needed new allies: he could turn only to the anti-Redmond nationalists. Events had conspired to give them a measure of common ground. Some of the writers and apolitical intellectuals who had shown sympathy with the labour movement during the lock-out — Patrick Pearse, Thomas MacDonagh and Joseph Plunkett — were members of the Irish Republican Brotherhood (IRB), a secret society pledged to the overthrow, by insurrection if necessary, of British rule in Ireland. (Moribund for years, the IRB by 1914 was a tightly knit, effective organisation, which had succeeded in infiltrating bodies like the Gaelic League and the Gaelic Athletic Association and, most important of all, the Irish Volunteers — now almost 200,000 strong and partially armed since a successful gun-running exploit in July.) Another Irish Volunteer and IRB member, Eamonn Ceannt, was also a prominent Sinn Féiner who had publicly disassociated himself from Griffith's attacks on the labour movement during the lockout. The threat of partition had made even Griffith try to bridge the gap with labour, but it was with the extremists of the IRB that Connolly sought an alliance. Although he had little in common with the largely bourgeois leadership, many of whom had a romantic and mystical approach to revolution which made him impatient, it was enough for the moment that they were hardline republicans who might provide the means to break the connection with Britain. Connolly was now convinced that Irish independence was a prerequisite for socialist success.

Through William O'Brien a meeting was arranged on 9 September with a number of radical nationalists. Connolly did not know which of those present were in the IRB, but they included Pearse, MacDonagh, Plunkett and Ceannt. The chair was taken by Tom Clarke, the man largely responsible (with his friend Seán MacDermott, also present) for resuscitating the IRB. It was agreed at the meeting that plans for insurrection should be made: two sub-committees were planned, one to make contact with Germany, the other to set up an open anti-recruiting propaganda organisation.

Redmond helped to stiffen the revolutionaries' resolve. On 20 September he called on the Irish Volunteers to fight overseas for Britain. His appeal precipitated a split. Eleven thousand men, under the leadership of Professor Eoin Mac Néill, retained the name Irish Volunteers; 170,000 others followed Redmond. When in October the Irish Volunteers were reorganised, key positions went to Pearse, MacDonagh, Plunkett and other IRB members. Mac Néill, not himself a member, had no knowledge of the allegiance of many of his comrades. With them in positions of power in the armed Volunteers and Connolly in control of the ICA, revolution had suddenly become a serious possibility.

6
Desperation

1

Connolly's political manoeuvrings had to be conducted alongside his full-time job as Larkin's trustee. Larkin had left the ITGWU administration in a dreadful state; the lockout had resulted in a pile of debts; the insurance fund was virtually insolvent; and membership had slumped. Connolly tackled these practical problems efficiently, introduced the necessary administrative reforms and devised means of raising money. The *Irish Worker* also underwent changes; it became his mouthpiece.

From the beginning he had made it clear that the ITGWU was to be as committed as its leader. Across the front of Liberty Hall was spread a banner which read: 'We serve neither King nor Kaiser — but Ireland.' Connolly became president of the anti-recruitment propaganda body, the Irish Neutrality League, set up, said its manifesto,

> for the purpose of defining Ireland's present attitude towards the Anglo-German war as one of neutrality, watching Ireland's interests at every phase of the war, preventing employers from coercing men to enlist, inculcating the view that true patriotism requires Irishmen to remain at home.

From October on, it held a number of anti-recruiting meetings, but because of lack of public support it fell apart after only a few months. The understanding with other nationalists also encountered early problems: Connolly was rebuffed when he sought ICA affiliation with the reorganised Irish Volunteers, to many of whom he seemed too dangerous and extreme. Connolly, greatly annoyed, concluded that the moderates were in control, but Volunteer politics were not as simple as that.

There were three distinct elements. The majority were separatist, anti-war and in favour of physical force only as a last resort against conscription in Ireland. Most of the few hundred IRB infiltrators (of whom Bulmer Hobson — Mac Néill's right-hand man — was the most influential) wanted a revolution against Britain when the moment was favourable, but felt bound by their constitution and their common sense, which directed that they should revolt only when backed by the majority of the Irish people. The third element was a small group who wanted revolution at all costs. Connolly, not knowing whom to trust, was suspicious of all. He and Pearse, though, were developing a mutual respect. The lockout and Connolly's writings — particularly *Labour in Irish History* and his articles in the *Irish Worker* — had aroused in Pearse an interest in social questions that by now was permeating his political consciousness. He never became a socialist, but he did make concessions to Connolly's belief in common ownership. Connolly reviewed one of his publications in December and expressed his pleasure at finding him 'so widely sympathetic to the struggles of the workers'. Pearse was a fine speaker and prolific writer, and, unlike most of his IRB fellows, who preferred to stay behind the scenes, he preached the gospel of revolution as strongly and openly as Connolly. In spite of all this, Connolly was not quick to drop his suspicions about the nationalist revolutionaries, whose temper and resolve he doubted. Pearse and his kind had always had enough to eat.

His impatience with the Volunteers' moderation
was heightened when Captain Robert Monteith, their most proficient military instructor, was dismissed from his government job and told to leave Dublin. 'If I had the handling of this matter,' Connolly told him, 'I would put you in position in Dublin, turn out every Volunteer in the city, and say to the government "Now come and take him." Tell Hobson this and if necessary I'll turn out the Citizen Army. That would stop all these deportation orders.' The Volunteers did not share Connolly's taste for confrontation: Monteith left Dublin. Connolly organised a protest meeting and urged those present to pledge themselves never to give up the fight until Ireland was a republic.

He always enjoyed living dangerously, and now his anti-war propaganda drew the authorities down on him. The *Irish Worker* was censored in early December, but Connolly published the banned editorial as a leaflet.

> Yes, my Lord and gentlemen [it concluded], our cards are on the table! If you leave us at liberty we will kill your recruiting, save our poor boys from your slaughterhouse, and blast your hopes of Empire. If you strike at, imprison or kill us, out of our prisons or graves we will still evoke a spirit that will thwart you and, mayhap, raise a force that will destroy you. We defy you! Do your worst.

The whole paper was suppressed in the following month.

2

Unable to find an Irish firm to take on the production of a banned paper, Connolly went to Glasgow after Christmas and found there old SLP friends who were willing to print the *Irish Worker* and smuggle it into Ireland. He did not moderate his views. In an article at the end of January 1915 he illustrated in graphic terms the inevitable atrocity of war but explained that it might nevertheless be justified: 'It may well be that in the progress of events the working class of Ireland may be called upon to face the stern necessity of taking the sword (or rifle) against the class whose rule has brought upon them and upon the world the hellish horror of the present European war.' (While revolutionaries like Pearse were carried away with romantic ideas about the glamour of revolution, Connolly's realism and army experience did not permit of sentimentality.) 'No,' he concluded, 'there is no such thing as humane or civilised war! War may be forced upon a subject race or subject class to put an end to subjection of race, of class, or sex. When so waged it must be waged thoroughly and relentlessly, but with no delusions as to its elevating nature, or civilising methods.'

Within a few weeks the police discovered the contraband arrangement and seized the whole consignment of the issue of 20 February 1915 as it was being unloaded from the ship. Connolly had to look elsewhere for a forum. In March he published in the *International Socialist Review* an article giving his explanation of why there had been no collective action by socialists to stop the war — the main blame for which lay with England's determination to protect her naval and hence commercial world supremacy. Germany had threatened that supremacy, and Britain had reacted. Connolly wanted to see Britain defeated and the seas free to all nations equally. (It has been questioned whether his allocation of guilt was simple anti-British feeling or a desire to counterbalance successful British propaganda in the minds of his American readers and also to assert, as a native of Britain, his freedom from the chauvinism he was deploring.

Evidence that, in private, he condemned the Germans [128] as being as bad as the British supports this view.) His analysis of the failure of resolve in the socialist movement was clear, as was his unshaken faith in industrial unionism:

> The failure of European Socialism to avert the war is primarily due to the divorce between the industrial and political movements of Labor. The Socialist voter, as such, is helpless between elections. He requires to organize power to enforce the mandate of the elections, and the *only power he can so organize is economic power* — the power to stop the wheels of commerce.

No amount of space in foreign publications would spread the word in Ireland: Connolly could no longer write honestly for *Forward* without bringing about its suppression: he desperately needed a paper of his own again. In February 1915 he discovered an old but serviceable printing press in Dublin, squashed a protest from a union member nervous of the consequences of publishing sedition from Liberty Hall, and produced on 29 May the first issue of the resurrected *Workers' Republic*.

Years of ascetic devotion to his cause had made him a formidable worker, and he was in his prime. Although his chief purpose, in the paper and in his speeches, was to encourage recruitment into the ICA rather than the British army, Connolly continued to stress his internationalism. At a meeting held on the day after the first issue of his new paper fraternal greetings were extended to workers in every country 'who are striving for the emancipation of their class'. Nor did he allow his revolutionary aspirations to divert him from his work for the labour movement. He continued to seize opportunities to secure wage rises for his members — through strikes when necessary — and worked too, though to little effect, for the strengthening of the Irish Labour Party. From platform and press he deplored the erosion of Irish liberties resulting from the Defence of the Realm Act (DORA), under which anti-recruitment meetings were suppressed, speakers prosecuted, restrictions imposed on trade union activities, and the banner removed from Liberty Hall.

Overriding all other concerns, though, was his yearning for revolution. Nora Connolly had been sent to America just before Christmas 1914 on an errand which, she was told, would mean treason charges against Clarke, MacDermott, Countess Markievicz and Connolly himself if discovered, but the close co-operation between Connolly and the IRB implicit in that action did not last. The IRB were about their business of strengthening their position within the Volunteers and trying to secure German aid for insurrection. Connolly was excluded from their councils, but they used him when they could. When they began to organise, as a massive republican demonstration, the funeral of the exiled Fenian, Jeremiah O'Donovan Rossa (whose body was being sent back from America), Connolly was persuaded by Clarke to contribute an article to the commemorative programme. He made his position clear:

> The Irish Citizen Army in its constitution pledges its members to fight for a Republican Freedom for Ireland. Its members are, therefore, of the number who believe that at the call of duty they may have to lay down their lives for Ireland, and have so trained themselves that at the worst the laying down of their lives shall constitute the starting point of another glorious tradition – a tradition that will keep alive the soul of the nation.

The ICA attended the funeral alongside the Volunteers

and heard Pearse deliver a powerful graveside oration [130] that matched Connolly's strength of commitment to revolution. For all Connolly's mistrust of mysticism, he was moved by the ceremony. In the *Workers' Republic* of the following week he wrote that the funeral seemed to come on a 'mission of divine uplifting and deliverance':

> The mist and doubts, the corruption and poisons, the distrust and the treacheries, were blown away, and the true men and women of Ireland saw with pleasure the rally of the nation to the olden ideas — saw the real people of the country solemnly bearing witness to the faith and wisdom of those who had 'fought a good fight, and kept the faith'. . . . Will the rallied Irish people stand fast as well as he whom they honoured?

3

It was now a year since the meeting at which the insurrection compact had been made. In that time IRB plans had run into a number of obstacles. Connolly attributed the delay to a failure of nerve and served warnings in the *Workers' Republic* that, if necessary, the ICA would fight alone:

> The Irish Citizen Army will only co-operate in a forward movement. The moment that forward movement ceases it reserves to itself the right to step out of the alignment, and advance by itself if needs be, in an effort to plant the banner of freedom one reach further towards its goal.

It was not an idle threat. The ICA remained small, but Connolly had done a great deal to make it a disciplined force. Training had been stepped up under Connolly's talented chief of staff, Michael Mallin, who, like Connolly, had served in the British army. The ICA had some arms (some stolen), and a rifle- range was installed in Liberty Hall. Battle exercises were held. Both Connolly and Mallin wrote regular articles in the *Workers' Republic* analysing the lessons to be learned from foreign insurrections of the previous century. Connolly's personal qualities inspired strong loyalty, and there could be no doubt that a substantial number of the 200-odd ICA men would follow him into rebellion. He was also expanding his reserve force, helped, as he gleefully pointed out, by a number of lockouts on the docks which enabled men who normally had no free evenings to come to Liberty Hall for training.

Impatient though he was for action, Connolly was well aware of the difference between 11,000 Volunteers and the tiny ICA. The *Workers' Republic* revealed him alternately sanguine and pessimistic about joint action. In mid-November depression was the keynote:

O, we latter-day Irish are great orators, and great singers, and great reciters, and great at cheering heroic sentiments about revolution. But we are not revolutionists. Not by a thousand miles! ... We strictly confine ourselves to killing John Bull with our mouths.

In a speech in late November he argued

that the saying 'England's difficulty is Ireland's opportunity,' has been heard on a thousand platforms in Ireland. England was in no small difficulty, but since England got into difficulties the phrase has never been heard or mentioned. If Ireland did not act now the name of this generation should in mercy to itself be expunged from the records of Irish history.

His impatience was further increased by new fears,

shared with the Volunteers, that conscription might [132] be forced on Ireland, and he spoke with Pearse at a large protest meeting towards the end of 1915. Connolly noted angrily in the *Workers' Republic* that economic conscription was being used instead; men were being sacked to persuade them to enlist:

> Under the forms of political freedom the souls of men are subjected to the cruellest tyranny in the world — recruiting has become a great hunting party with the souls and bodies of men as the game to be hunted and trapped.

The insurrection would not simply be a reaction; it had a great objective:

> We want and must have economic conscription in Ireland for Ireland. Not the conscription of men by hunger to compel them to fight for the power that denies them the right to govern their own country, but the conscription by an Irish nation of all the resources of the nation . . . that Ireland may live and bear upon her fruitful bosom the greatest number of the freest people she has ever known. . . .
>
> Whosoever in future speaks for Ireland, calls Irishmen to arms, should remember that the first duty of Irishmen is to reconquer their country — to take it back from those whose sole right to its ownership is based upon conquest.
>
> If the arms of the Irish Volunteers and Irish Citizen Army is the military weapon of, the economic conscription of its land and wealth is the material basis for, that reconquest.

Connolly's personal hatred of war was as great as ever. When, in December 1915, he read in an article by Pearse on the European war: 'The old heart of the earth needed to be warmed with the red wine of the battle-fields,' Connolly retorted in his paper:

No, we do not think that the old heart of the earth needs to be warmed with the red wine of millions of lives. We think anyone who does is a blithering idiot. We are sick of such teaching, and the world is sick of such teaching.

Talks between Connolly and the Volunteers foundered: Mac Néill would not accept Connolly's view that any arrests of ICA or Volunteer members should be met with armed resistance. ICA/IRB meetings had been not much more successful, since the IRB, though eager to convince Connolly that they meant business, were not prepared to let him in on their specific plans.

Connolly's anxiety for speedy action was conditioned by his antipathy to fighting a Britain which was at peace and free to concentrate its military strength on Ireland. In time of peace, he said, he would confine himself to the peaceful work of industrial unionism. In time of war it was right to fight for freedom. In this he differed from Pearse, who was not looking for a winnable battle but a gesture. Connolly did not share the sacrificial mood; he believed, at this stage, that there was a chance of victory.

The IRB were becoming seriously worried by Connolly's vocal public militancy. While in December he had sounded enthusiastic about an alliance ('[There] is growing the feeling of identity of interests between the forces of real nationalism and of Labour which we have long worked and hoped for in Ireland'), in the following month his urgency was at its peak: 'The time for Ireland's battle is NOW the place for Ireland's battle is HERE.'

This outburst finally convinced the IRB that unless he was included in their counsels he might take precipitate action, fail, and thereby cause the disbanding of the Volunteers. He was persuaded to attend a meeting of the IRB Military Council — Pearse, Plunkett, Ceannt, Clarke and MacDermott (MacDonagh was co-opted later) — and, after long negotiations, he was convinced that there would definitely be a rebellion on Easter Sunday, 23 April 1916. He agreed to wait and join with them and was co-opted onto the council.

Connolly sank his doubts. In the *Workers' Republic* he wrote:

> The issue is clear, and we have done our part to clear it. Nothing we can say now can add point to the argument we have put before our readers in the past few months; nor shall we continue to labour the point.
>
> In solemn acceptance of our duty and the great responsibilities attached thereto, we have planted the seed in the hope that ere many of us are much older, it will ripen into action. For the moment and hour of that ripening, that fruitful blessed day of days, we are ready. Will it find you ready too?

In throwing in his lot with the Volunteers, Connolly had to accept that any insurrection in which they were jointly involved would not be in the name of a socialist future. He had to make concessions. The workers of Ireland were flocking into the British army, not the ICA. They had let him down. 'For the sake of a few paltry shillings, Irish workers have sold their country in the hour of their country's greatest need and greatest hope.' He saw self-interest binding all classes of the population to the Empire. The trade union movement as a whole had little sympathy with his militarism, and even within his own union there were rumblings about his preaching revolution. They were complaining too about the use of Liberty Hall for training and the storage of arms.

Between Connolly's decision in January to join

with the Volunteers and the actual outbreak of the insurrection in April he continued his normal union work, negotiating with employers and other unions, dealing with strikes and editing his paper. He even found time to call a truce with the Catholic Church, following a sympathetic address by a Capuchin, Father Lawrence, on social matters with which, Connolly said, he had no fundamental difference. 'The Church recognises that if she does not move with the people, the people will move without her.'

His best energies were going into the organisation of the ICA, which now provided an armed guard at Liberty Hall to protect its military stores, its bomb factory, its printing press and its leader — whose arrest was ever more likely.

It was a measure of the weakness of the British authorities in Dublin Castle that Connolly managed to go on for so long openly preaching sedition. Insurgents had in the past waited too long, he said in a speech on 6 March. 'To us a glorious opportunity has come.' On 18 March: 'Her sons and daughters must hold life itself as of little value when weighed against the preservation of even the least important work of her separate individuality as a nation.' His defiance did not stop at words. On 24 March he was called to a shop beside Liberty Hall which was being raided for subversive publications. When the policeman failed to produce a search-warrant (unnecessary under DORA) Connolly drew his revolver and said: 'Then drop those papers, or I'll drop you.' Thinking the Liberty Hall press might be next, he mobilised the ICA. From all over the city poured 'working men with grimy faces and dirty working clothes rushing excitedly through the streets with rifle in hand and bandolier across shoulders'. Within an hour 150 were at Liberty Hall. On 26 March a play by Connolly, *Under Which Flag,* was performed in Liberty Hall (he wrote one other in

America), which told of a young man torn between [136] the British army and the IRB, for which he opted finally.

From then on Liberty Hall was guarded day and night. Connolly left Countess Markievicz's house and moved a bed into his office. On 8 April the *Workers' Republic* announced that the green flag of Ireland would be hoisted over Liberty Hall on 16 April 'as a rallying point of our forces and embodiment of all our hopes. Where better could that flag fly than over the unconquered citadel of the Irish working class, Liberty Hall, the fortress of the militant working class of Ireland?'

> We are out for Ireland for the Irish. But who are the Irish? . . . The Irish working class, the only secure foundation upon which a free nation can be reared. The cause of labour is the cause of Ireland, the cause of Ireland is the cause of labour.

The green flag was too much for the peaceable members of the ITGWU, who, quite naturally, had been feeling more and more uneasy. Connolly told them he would resign rather than give in, but soothed them with the assurance that the ICA would shortly leave Liberty Hall and 'probably never return'.

He appeared in uniform for the first time on Palm Sunday (16 April) to inspect his troops, and, after bugles, drums, pipes and salutes, the flag was raised. Later that day Connolly gave a talk on street fighting in which he referred to the imminent rising: 'If we win, we'll be great heroes; but if we lose, we'll be the greatest scoundrels the country ever produced.' He asked if anyone present wished to withdraw; no one did.

In the week leading up to the insurrection the conspirators suffered a number of setbacks. The promised German arms ship arrived ahead of time off Tralee and was scuttled to avoid capture of the weapons. The Irish nationalist and ex-British colonial official [137] Sir Roger Casement was arrested when he landed in Kerry on Good Friday from a German submarine. Mac Néill at last realised that a revolution was imminent and countermanded Pearse's orders for manoeuvres for all Volunters on Easter Sunday. Early on Easter Sunday the Military Council met at Liberty Hall. They agreed on a postponement until Easter Monday in order to give the minimum of time to remobilise the Volunteers, who had stood down. Further delay was impossible; the government's knowledge of the attempt to import German arms made arrests likely. Connolly's Sunday afternoon was spent in parading at the head of the Citizen Army — which had turned out according to plan. The Proclamation of the Irish Republic was run off on the presses of the *Workers' Republic*.

4

About 120 of the ICA turned out on Easter Monday, 24 April 1916. Mac Néill's countermanding order struck a heavy blow to the Volunteer contingent; with confusion in the ranks their total forces — now combined as the Irish Republican Army — amounted to around 1,000 (although more turned up during the Rising). The start—stop—start orders had left the provinces largely unmobilised, and the action was virtually confined to Dublin.

Pearse had been appointed President of the Provisional Government and Commander-in-Chief. Connolly was Commandant-General of the Dublin forces. By now he had no illusions about the outcome of the Rising. As he walked down the steps of Liberty Hall he told William O'Brien the rebels were going out to be slaughtered.

The plan was to seize strategic points in Dublin and [138] hold them as long as possible. ICA men were to take Dublin Castle; troops led by Mallin and Countess Markievicz (a lieutenant in the ICA) were to occupy St Stephen's Green. The mixed headquarters force of fewer than 150 Volunteers and ICA were to occupy the General Post Office, which dominated Sackville Street, the main thoroughfare of Dublin. They set off at noon, headed by Pearse and Connolly — both in uniform, Connolly's the dark green with slouch hat of the ICA — and Plunkett, Clarke and MacDermott. Only some of the men rose to a uniform; many had only a cap or badge as a symbol. Their weapons included rifles, shotguns, picks and spades — some even bore pikes. As they reached the GPO Connolly shouted: 'Left turn! Charge!' and they poured in, ejecting staff and customers.

From the first moment Connolly took the leadership, detailing men to smash windows, fortify them and barricade the doors. He had no competition from the other leaders. Clarke and MacDermott had played a decisive part in organising the IRB for rebellion, but they had no personal military ambitions. Plunkett was dying of consumption. Pearse, although he was nominally in charge, gratefully recognised Connolly's superior military skills and left him to direct affairs throughout the Rising.

The green flag and the green, white and orange tricolour were raised over the GPO, and Connolly accompanied Pearse outside to hear him read the Proclamation of the Republic, signed by the seven members of the Military Council. Although the Proclamation did not mention socialism by name, it contained a declaration of the right of the people of Ireland to the ownership of Ireland which could be construed as socialist if subsequent interpreters of it so wished. It also made specific commitments to religious and civil liberty, equal rights and equal opportunities to all citizens, and women's suffrage. It has frequently been adduced as evidence that Connolly had sacrificed socialism to nationalism; yet, had he ever been in a position to implement it, there was enough scope within its generalisations to justify his prosecution of his own programme.

Although the crowd that heard the reading was indifferent, Connolly was moved. Taking Pearse's hand he said: 'Thanks be to God, Pearse, we have lived to see this day.'

Connolly's competence and decisiveness as a commander were in evidence throughout the Rising. It was he who made the decisions, solved the problems, sent men to outposts, inspected their barricades, maintained a correspondence with other commandants and kept up morale by exhortation, praise, bullying, anger and encouragement. Pearse described him as 'the guiding spirit of our resistance'. Michael Collins, a young Volunteer later to be a great military leader, said of him: 'There was an air of earthy directness about Connolly. It impressed me. I would have followed him through hell.'

He was not eternally the hard man. Shocked by the mass looting of shops in Sackville Street he sent a detachment of men to stop it. When they failed he announced his intention of sending out another party to shoot some of the looters as an example, but could not bring himself to do it. They were, after all, of the very people Connolly was prepared to die for; his companions were prepared to die for Ireland.

British forces, handicapped by the public holiday, took time to get into battle order. Fire-power was first concentrated on the rebel outposts, and for the first two days the GPO contingent was troubled only by snipers. It has been frequently said (though never proved) that Connolly had always held that the British would limit themselves to small arms, since no capitalist state would use heavy weapons and risk destroying property. If so, this illusion crumbled when, on Wednesday morning, a gun-boat on the river shelled Liberty Hall which, though empty, was regarded by the authorities — in a tribute which Connolly would have appreciated — as 'the centre of social anarchy in Ireland, the brain of every riot and disturbance'. Even the arrival of artillery was the occasion for perverse optimism from Connolly: clearly the British were expecting German aid for the rebels.

By Wednesday afternoon British troops had loosely encircled the GPO. Shells were lobbed into Sackville Street, igniting buildings. As the troops drew nearer on Thursday rifle and artillery fire increased and the fire began to spread. Connolly led a sortie to try to set up a barricade to the west. He received a flesh wound; then a bullet smashed his left ankle. He dragged himself close to the GPO and was carried in on a stretcher. A captured British army doctor operated and managed to keep the worst of the agony at bay through morphine.

Even after a night of pain he refused to stay out of things. He was wheeled on a bed into the front hall, where he dictated to his devoted secretary, Winifred Carney (a suffragette when she first began to work for him in Belfast), an address which was read to the GPO garrison. To boost morale it spoke of non-existent successes in the Rising and ended:

> Courage, boys, we are winning, and in the hour of our victory let us not forget the splendid women who have everywhere stood by us and cheered us on. Never had man or woman a grander cause, never was a cause more grandly served.

He certainly knew that they could not stay long in the building — British artillery was too close — but he remained in good spirits and continued to direct activities. Late that afternoon, with the building on fire, complete evacuation was ordered. Connolly and Pearse both refused to leave until everyone else was clear, and Connolly was then carried on a stretcher into the street, Winifred Carney refusing to leave his side.

They took refuge in a nearby house, from which, on Saturday morning, they sent out a message of surrender. Although Clarke and Pearse had wanted to go on, the prospect of further casualties made the others disagree. Connolly could not stand the thought of his men being burned to death. The surrender had to be unconditional. By Saturday afternoon, his ankle now gangrenous, Connolly was in custody in an infirmary in Dublin Castle.

5

Connolly knew that he and the other signatories of the Proclamation would be shot. On Monday 1 May he made his confession to a Catholic priest; the following day he received communion. It was a logical step, though it has been variously interpreted as anything from proof that he was always a believing Catholic to proof that he had abandoned his socialism. Only a couple of weeks before the Rising a friend had asked if he ever believed there was anything on the other side. 'Oh no,' answered Connolly, with a laugh, 'I'm afraid I haven't time to be thinking about all that kind of thing just now.' On his hospital bed he had time to think, as did other non-practising Catholics who were to be executed and chose to be received back into the Church. He may have regained his faith; he may merely have been taking a prudent precaution against finding after all that there was a God; he may even have been ensuring that his doctrines could less easily be dismissed as atheism after his death. His [142] motives are unimportant. At the very least, it was a gesture of solidarity with the people for whom he had laboured all his life.

He was a mellow, pleasant man during his last days. His captors spoke warmly of his considerateness. With Lillie and Nora he was cheerful — proud of the courage shown by the rebels and particularly proud that his sixteen-year-old son had been among those imprisoned, though badly upset when he heard that a good friend, the pacifist Francis Sheehy-Skeffington, had been summarily executed, having been arrested while trying to stop looting.

He was court-martialled on Tuesday 9 May and condemned to death. His statement to the court martial defended the aim of the Rising, which had succeded 'in proving that Irishmen are ready to die endeavouring to win for Ireland those national rights which the British Government has been asking them to die to win for Belgium. As long as that remains the case, the cause of Irish freedom is safe.' He wished to make no defence except on the charge of causing wanton cruelty to prisoners. He said nothing in his statement about socialism — there was no reason to do so. He had fought along with the others in a common cause — an Irish republic; his personal vision of the form that republic should take was available in countless pieces of writing. He is said to have lamented to Nora that socialists would not understand his actions: 'They will all forget I am an Irishman.' Perhaps he did not realise that the Irish would forget he was a socialist.

In the early hours of Friday 12 May Lillie and Nora were brought to see him; he was to be shot at dawn. Lillie was in tears. 'But your beautiful life, James. Your beautiful life.'

'Hasn't it been a full life, Lillie, and isn't this a good end?'

After receiving the last rites he was driven to Kilmainham jail, where he was asked if he would pray for the men about to shoot him. 'Yes, Sir, I'll pray for all brave men who do their duty according to their lights.' Unable to stand, he was shot sitting on a rough deal box.[36]

'He was', said the surgeon who attended him, 'the bravest man I have ever known.'

6

Connolly's execution was the fifteenth. Public reaction to the shooting of an injured man helped to stop any more; the other ninety-seven condemned prisoners were spared. He was assumed with the other dead men into Irish patriotic martyrology, his greatest intellectual contribution, hibernicised Marxism, overlooked or purposely ignored. He left behind a labour movement quickly dominated by respectable men; virulent anti-Communism in Catholic Ireland made Marx a name to be feared. As a patriot he was venerated in debate, on grand occasions and in the classroom — in highly selective terms. Outside of labour circles, only the tiny Irish Communist Party remembered anything of what he had written. Not until the late 1960s did he appeal again to a wider audience, when the appositeness of his remarks on Ulster brought him to the attention of the Civil Rights movement.

He fared little better abroad. As he had expected, most British socialists found his rebellion incomprehensible. How could the proponent of class warfare die for a bourgeois revolution? In Europe there was a little, but only a little, more understanding. Lenin was one of the few socialists anywhere who applauded the Easter Rising — and he, it would seem, had never heard of James Connolly.

Although many of his contemporaries knew he was

a great man (and that of all the leaders of the Rising [144] he had the best mind), most of them were bewildered as to what had led him — the indispensable one — to sacrifice himself on the altar of nationalism. Had he himself not warned them of the danger inherent in the achievement of national independence?:

> If you remove the English army tomorrow and hoist the green flag over Dublin Castle, unless you set about the organisation of the socialist republic, your efforts would be in vain. England would still rule . . . through her capitalists . . . to your ruin, even while your lips offered hypocritical homage at the shrine of that Freedom whose cause you betrayed.

Of the many reasons that have been put forward, two of the most plausible are (1) that his natural impatience, which led him to change parties and places so frequently, led him, when all options were closed, into desperate action, and (2) that he realised that syndicalism in a hostile environment is unworkable, and believed that a British victory in the war would shore up the capitalist state indefinitely, and so seized the only revolutionary moment available to him.

What is rarely taken into account is the heat of his hatred for the originators, perpetrators and exploiters of the poverty and degradation he saw all around him. In his last months it drove him to distraction to see the Dublin poor, humiliated in 1914, going out to die abroad for imperialism, at the behest of those who had crushed them. Hate inspired the article he wrote in response to a particularly noisome recruiting line — that the Dublin slums were more unhealthy than the Flanders trenches. Who were the recruiters? he asked: those who gloated over the plight of the locked-out workers and set the police to baton them. 'The trenches safer than the Dublin slums! We may yet see the day that the trenches will be safer for these gentry than any part of Dublin.' Pearse himself said to a [145] friend: 'He will never be satisfied until he goads us into action, and then he will think most of us are too moderate, and want to guillotine half of us.'[37] And a week before the Rising Connolly told the Citizen Army:

> In the event of victory, hold on to your rifles, as those with whom we are fighting may stop before our goal is reached. We are out for economic as well as political liberty.

Mere words, perhaps — but indicative of a great sense of outrage and betrayal. A quarter-century of work had yielded little fruit in Britain or America. And Ireland too, in the end to prove impervious to his message and to abandon it for the King's shilling, made a mockery of all the sacrifice that he and, through him, his family had made.

Perhaps he was best understood by the liberal Home Ruler Tom Kettle, who recruited for the British army and was himself killed on the western front. Kettle, though in so much the antithesis of Connolly, was a gifted and sensitive man, with insights into the passions of others. Asked by a friend, soon after the Rising, to account for Connolly's end, Kettle quoted this poem by Francis Adams, speaking the last stanza twice:

> 'Tis not when I am here,
>   In these homeless homes,
> Where sin and shame and disease
>   And foul death comes.
>
> 'Tis not when heart and brain
>   Would be still and forget
> Men and women and children
>   Dragged down to the pit:

But when I hear them declaiming
  Of 'liberty', 'order', and 'law',
The husk-hearted Gentleman
  And the mud-hearted Bourgeois,

That a sombre hateful desire
  Burns up slow in my breast
To wreck the great guilty Temple
  And give us rest![38]

Suggested Further Reading

The definitive biography of Connolly is yet to be written, but C. Desmond Greaves, *The Life and Times of James Connolly*, London 1961, has a wealth of useful detail (although his Stalinism makes his interpretations suspect) and Samuel Levenson, *James Connolly*, London 1973 (unduly dependent on Greaves), is more readable and makes use of some of the O'Brien collection mentioned below. Other important works include:

Cardoza, Nancy, *Maud Gonne*, London 1979

Connolly, James, *Labour in Ireland*, Dublin and London 1917

Cronin, Seán, *Young Connolly*, Dublin 1978

Edwards, Owen Dudley, *The Mind of an Activist – James Connolly*, Dublin 1971

Edwards, Owen Dudley, and Ransom, Bernard, ed., *James Connolly: Selected Political Writings*, London 1973

Edwards, Ruth Dudley, *Patrick Pearse: The Triumph of Failure*, London 1977

Gaughan, J. Anthony, *Thomas Johnson*, Dublin 1980

Larkin, Emmet, *James Larkin*, London 1965

Lyons, F. S. L., *Ireland Since the Famine*, London 1973

MacBride, Maud Gonne, *A Servant of the Queen*, London 1938

Marreco, Anne, *The Rebel Countess: The Life and Times of Countess Markievicz*, London 1967

O'Brien, Conor Cruise, *States of Ireland*, London 1972

O'Brien, Nora Connolly, *Portrait of a Rebel Father*, London 1975

O'Brien, William, *Forth the Banners Go*, ed. E. MacLysaght, Dublin 1969

O'Casey, Seán, *Drums Under the Window*, New York 1950

O'Faolain, Seán, *Constance Markievicz*, London 1934

Ransom, Bernard, *Connolly's Marxism*, London 1980

Reeves, Carl, and Barton, Ann, *James Connolly and the United States*, New Jersey 1978

Renshaw, Patrick, *The Wobblies*, London 1967

Ryan, Desmond, *James Connolly*, Dublin 1924, *Remembering Sion*, London 1934, *The Rising*, Dublin 1949

Ryan, W. P., *The Irish Labour Movement*, Dublin n.d.

Notes

To save space, the notes have been kept to a minimum. The vast majority of the published writings of Connolly quoted here can be found in Connolly, *op. cit.*, Edwards and Ransom, ed., *op. cit.*, or in the three-volume selection of his writings edited by Desmond Ryan and published in Dublin: *Socialism and Nationalism* (1948), *Labour and Easter Week* (1949) and *The Workers' Republic* (1951).

Another important source for this book is the William O'Brien collection in the National Library of Ireland, which includes all correspondence quoted here unless otherwise specified. Bernard Ransom's unpublished Edinburgh thesis, 'James Connolly and the Scottish Left, 1890–1916' (1975) has been of great value.

1. From the version in the Connolly Souvenir, Dublin 1919. For speculation about date of composition, see Reeves, *op. cit.*, 177.
2. See Ransom, 'James Connolly and the Scottish Left', 13, and Reeves and Barton, *op. cit.*, 10.
3. 3/7/'94.
4. Seán O'Casey, *op. cit.*, 22.
5. Quoted in Greaves, *op. cit.*, 73.
6. W. B. Yeats, *Autobiographies*, London 1926, 366.
7. J. Carstairs Matheson (pseudonym 'Sans Culotte') in *Justice*, 22/6/'01.
8. 9/6/'02.
9. 7/5/'05 to Jack Mulray; and see e.g. 28/8/'02 and n.d./3/'03 to Matheson and 11/2/'03 from Matheson.
10. Matheson to Connolly, 2/3/'07.
11. Connolly to Matheson, 8/4/'03.
12. *Ibid.*, 27/12/'05.
13. *Ibid.*
14. Matheson to Connolly, 9/12/'05.

15. *Ibid.*, 27/9/'08.
16. Connolly to Matheson, 7/5/'08.
17. Elizabeth Gurley Flynn, *I Speak My Own Piece*, New York 1955, 60.
18. Connolly to Matheson, 8/11/'08.
19. At various times he learned German and Italian to a level of fluency; he could read French; he learned a little Irish, and, it is thought, even some Arabic.
20. Ryan, *Remembering Sion*, 55—7.
21. 10/6/'09.
22. See Levenson, *op. cit.*, 180.
23. 30/1/'08.
24. Cathal O'Shannon, 'James Connolly: the Man and the Leader' in the James Connolly Commemoration Souvenir Pamphlet, Dublin, May 1930.
25. James Doherty in conversation with Owen Dudley Edwards.
26. Quoted in Nora Connolly O'Brien, *op. cit.*, 110.
27. J. Anthony Gaughan, *op. cit.*, 20.
28. Connolly to R. J. Hoskin, 14/6/'11.
29. Connolly to Edward Lynch, 23/5/'12.
30. William McMullen's introduction to Ryan, ed., *The Workers' Republic*.
31. Connolly to O'Brien, 29/7/'13.
32. *Ibid.*
33. P. H. Pearse, *Political Writings and Speeches*, Dublin 1962, 178—9.
34. O'Brien, *op. cit.*, 120.
35. Connolly to O'Brien, 7/10/'14.
36. Michael Tierney, *Eoin MacNeill*, Oxford 1981, 240.
37. Ryan, *The Rising*, 49.
38. 'Anarchists', quoted in Robert Lynd's introduction to Connolly, *Labour in Ireland*.

Index

Askwith, Sir George, 105
Aveling, Edward, 4, 13

Carney, Winifred, 140, 141
Carson, Sir Edward, 99, 108
Casement, Sir Roger, 137
Ceannt, Eamonn, 122, 123, 134
Chamberlain, Joseph, 33
Clarke, Tom, 123, 129, 134, 138
Collins, Michael, 139
Connolly, Aideen (daughter), 5
Connolly, Fiona (daughter), 57
Conolly, Ina (daughter), 23
Connolly, John (father), 1, 3, 35
Connolly, John (brother), 1, 4
Connolly, Lillie (wife), 3, 4, 14,
    15, 27, 37, 50, 51, 69, 71,
    84–5, 88, 142
Connolly, Máire (daughter), 27
Connolly, Mary (mother), 1, 3
Connolly, Mona (daughter), 5, 50,
    51
Connolly, Nora (daughter), 5, 87,
    88, 92, 129, 142
Connolly, Roderick (son), 37
Connolly, Thomas (brother), 1

Daly, P. T., 92–3, 104, 119
Davitt, Michael, 9, 33
Debs, Eugene, 52
De Leon, Daniel, 40–1, 43, 44,
    46, 47, 48–9, 51–9, 53, 54–9,
    61, 63, 75

Flynn, Elizabeth Gurley, 86

Galway, Mary, 91–2

George V, 89, 105
Gladstone, W. E., 8
Glasier, Bruce, 36
Gonne, Maud, 23, 25, 26, 28, 32,
    33–4, 35, 85, 86, 112
Griffith, Arthur, 33, 34, 35, 64,
    122

Hardie, Keir, 6, 10, 12, 17, 27, 37,
    62, 105
Hobson, Bulmer, 125
Hyndman, Henry, 5, 13

Kane, Fr, 74–7, 86
Kautsky, Karl, 36, 37, 38, 41
Kettle, Tom, 145

Lalor, James Fintan, 21, 73
Lansbury, George, 13, 107
Larkin, Delia, 105
Larkin, James, 70, 71, 81–5,
    88–93, 97–8, 101, 103–10,
    114, 117–21, 124
Lawrence, Fr, 135
Lenin, V. I., 120, 143
Leo XIII, 77
Leslie, John, 4, 5, 9, 10, 13, 87
Lloyd George, David, 108
Luxemburg, Rosa, 36
Lyng, Jack, 22, 50
Lyng, Murtagh, 22, 38–9
Lyng, Tom, 22, 46, 66

MacDermott, Seán, 123, 129, 134,
    138
MacDonagh, Tom, 122, 123, 134
MacErlean, Fr, 100

Mac Néill, Eoin, 123, 125, 133, 137
Mallin, Michael, 130–1, 138
Mao Tse-tung, 21
Markievicz, Constance, 105, 112, 129, 136, 138
Marx, Karl, 4, 26, 48, 67
Matheson, J. Carstairs, 41, 45, 46, 49, 50, 51, 55, 57, 58, 62, 67, 74
Millerand, Alexandre, 36
Milligan, Alice, 21, 22, 24
Milligan, Ernest, 22
Monteith, Captain Robert, 126
Morris, William, 4
Mulray, Jack, 47, 50
Murphy, William Martin, 103, 104, 106, 112

O'Brien, Daniel, 22, 29, 44
O'Brien, Pat, 33
O'Brien, Thomas, 22
O'Brien, William, 22, 42, 46, 67, 68–70, 72, 88, 89, 97, 101, 102, 104, 118, 122, 123, 137
O'Casey, Seán, 16, 33, 80, 82
O'Donovan Rossa, Jeremiah, 129
O'Leary, John, 33
Owen, Robert, 79

Parnell, Charles Stewart, 2, 8, 9, 10
Pearse, Patrick, 111–12, 122, 123, 125, 127, 130, 132, 133, 134, 137–9, 141, 145
Plunkett, Joseph, 122, 123, 134, 138

Quinlan, Patrick, 53, 54

Redmond, John, 33, 34, 121, 122, 123
Redmond, William, 33
Russell, George ('AE'), 106, 107, 111

Shaw, George Bernard, 107, 111
Sheehy-Skeffington, Francis, 142

Tone, Theobald Wolfe, 22, 26, 27

Vandeleur, Arthur, 79
Victoria, Queen, 23, 34–5, 89

Walker, William, 87–8, 94
Walsh, Archbishop William, 107
White, Captain Jack, 114

Yeats, W. B., 23, 111

AN ILLUSTRATED HISTORY OF IRELAND

John Grenham

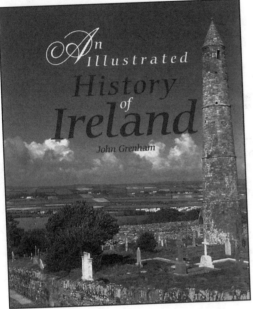

An *Illustrated History of Ireland* provides a fascinating account of the origins of the Irish people from prehistoric times to the present day. It tells of the effect of invasion, war, famine and emigration and how these have influenced the make up of Ireland and the Irish.

Illustrated throughout with full-colour photographs of landscapes, historic sites and artefacts, this book will be welcomed by Irish people at home and abroad.

| £5.99 | PAPERBACK | 0 7171 2553 X |